*ICE*

I really enjoyed the book. It makes total sense, the stories are excellent, and it applies to everything and every situation you might encounter.

—Anne | Sales Consultant

Thank you for asking me to read *Iceberg Selling*. I truly enjoyed it. Being a salesperson lights me up, and I resonated with so much of the book, and the learning objectives/takeaways are perfect for salespeople to get into action right away.

—Lynne | Business Development

I absolutely loved this book! It's as much about being a better salesperson as it could be about how to be a better person, a better spouse, parent…inspiring! The story about Tim and his dad really hit. How you demonstrate how to be disarming, allowing for walls to break down and truths to be exposed, is a great example of solution selling at its best!

—Steve | Account Executive

You got me fired up to apply Iceberg Selling to my own sales process. I don't use "empowered" lightly, but I genuinely feel reinvigorated to embrace a drivership mindset to take control of my story and success.

—Ben | Creative Producer/Consultant

The whole concept of sitting on the same side of the table is great and refreshing. We've taken that approach and tell all clients that "we're an extension of your team."

—Dave | Sales Director

# ICEBERG SELLING

# ICEBERG SELLING

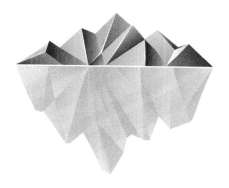

Become a Better Salesperson
by Looking Below the Surface

# KARL BECKER

First Printing 2023
ISBN 979-8-218-03566-2
Ebook ISBN 979-8-218-27025-4

Improving Sales Performance
improvingsalesperformance.com

Interior and cover design by Olivia M. Hammerman
(Indigo: Editing, Design, and More)

Illustrations by Leigh Thomas

*Dedicated to everyone in sales
who puts themselves out there every day.*

# Contents

# Introduction

## Why I Love Salespeople

**Salespeople are some of my favorite people in the world.** I really mean that.

You're the cornerstones of your company, the people who make your company successful and make sure everyone gets paid. You're driven and tenacious, and you never give up. In short, you're the kind of person I want to hang out with.

We as salespeople also create the revenue that enables people to buy their first homes, pay for their kids' college education, and care for their families. We put presents underneath the Christmas tree and food on the table, and we help the people who work at our companies do the same thing. Salespeople make the world go around.

You may not have envisioned being a salesperson when you were young, but from the beginning, you probably were already a communicator, a connector, a person who makes things happen. The awesome news is that, as a salesperson, you've found a place where those are the perfect skills for the job.

I bet you're a good salesperson.

I bet you're good at connecting with people. I bet you're the kind of person who knows how to create a vision and reality. You listen and truly understand people, and you move them closer to that vision. You're the type of person who takes concepts and distills them into accessible and even inspirational ideas. You are someone who other people want to be around. You've got a positive attitude. You see yourself as someone who can accomplish whatever you put your mind to.

And I bet you'd get even more juice, more motivation, more satisfaction with what you do every day if you could raise your game and become a great salesperson. This book is meant to inspire you and to arm you with a fresh approach that will help you make that jump. It's called Iceberg Selling.

Iceberg Selling is an approach that connects you with customers in powerful ways that set you apart from competitors. It creates a mental framework that, even if you put the smallest parts of it into practice, can lead to big, positive changes.

Selling this way helps you make your customers feel seen and understood. Which makes them want to interact with you more and more. It invites them to co-create solutions with you and pumps them up to see those solutions through to the end.

My goal in writing this book is to get you to the next level in your career, to pull you out of where you are now and show you how to get where you want to be. I'll tell you quick and memorable stories, talk about lessons learned, and share inspiration and best practices I've used in my career and life. I hope the mindset shifts and best practices I am about to show you light up your brain and get you thinking, *I can do this.* I hope the aha moments and lessons I share will make you want to commit them to memory and use them in your own unique approach to sales and life.

Because ultimately, this is a journey that you're going on yourself. Being better in sales starts with you. I can give you resources, and so can a lot of other people. But we're also going to talk about what you're playing for and how you can commit and recommit to what you want by applying Iceberg Selling to all your customer interactions.

## What Are You Playing For?

To go from good to great, you need to look under the surface of what you want. So, I'm going to ask you a question I'd like you to answer right now: Why are you in sales?

I'm in sales because I want the freedom to bet on myself. I want to be the one who charts my own course. Even though I believe in coming together and supporting teams, I'm an independent person. Ultimately, I run my own race, and I believe that most of us who are in sales run our own races too.

And of course I love the rush of the yes. *Yes, let's move forward. Yes, that's a great idea. Yes, let's do it.* I'm not ashamed to say I love the money too. There's nothing quite like hitting a huge commission, achieving a quarterly or annual bonus, and seeing a big check deposited in my account.

I bet you feel the same way. You might be in sales because you want to make things happen. You want to make a lot of money. You want to bet on yourself and see yourself win. You probably want to have an impact on your organization, your life, and your family's lives too. There's nothing wrong with any or all of that being your reason, but you should know your reason.

Sales can be really stressful, yet rewarding, and I find that people who know why they're in it and what they want to get out of it have a way better time becoming great salespeople. So, here's the follow-up question I like to ask: What are you playing for?

I like to ask questions like these and let the salespeople I coach sit with them and really think about them. Their answers always surprise me, impress me, inspire me, and make me smile. While we're all different, we all have similar things that we play for. Most likely, we are looking for a change in our life to a better state, whether that means offering more financial support for our spouse as they go back to school, paying for college, or having the ability to help a friend who needs it. Maybe we want to reward ourselves for all the hard work we do—whether it's with a trip, a new boat, a new car, a bigger house, or a favorite pair of shoes.

There are physical things we play for, but there are also the things that fulfill us emotionally. These are things like stability and security, freedom, and confidence in your ability to make a positive impact in the lives of other people. You get filled up by knowing you're creating the revenue your company needs to grow and support payroll. That kind of stuff can feel just as good, if not better, as an early retirement or a new car. The answer depends on you.

Whatever your motivation, I want to tell you right now it's completely okay. In fact, it's more than okay. It's incredible. It's yours, and I want you to own it.

Feeling connected to my friends, clients, and family is extremely important to me. One of the biggest things I play for is giving people I care about opportunities and support to get where they want to be faster. I'd like to share two personal examples to show how being in sales may also allow you to make things happen for yourself and others.

My friend Cindy is a consultant, and we've worked together for years. (By the way, her name isn't actually Cindy. I'll be using pseudonyms in this book to protect people's privacy.) Recently, she got divorced and had to take on a bigger workload to support herself and her children.

Cindy and I were working on a project together for the same client. She was running their marketing team, and I was running the sales team. I noticed that her computer setup was a mess. It was pretty old, the power cord was broken, and the battery had zero life left.

When I asked her about it, she said, "Yeah, this is an old computer. I'm saving up for a new one."

"Here's an idea," I said. "If my sales team hits our quarterly goal, we're going to get a new laptop for you and gift cards for your team."

My sales team could make higher bonuses as we achieved our sales goals, but the marketing team didn't have that kind of variable compensation. At the beginning of the quarter, the rest of the sales team and I shared with one another what we were playing for. Some people wanted new snow skis or tickets to visit family or a nice date night with their spouse.

I told my sales team we were playing for something else that quarter too—to support our marketing teammates. They were in, and true to our word, we made it happen. Everyone on the team reached their own goals and our goals for Cindy and the marketing team. It brought us all together, and it was all possible because of sales.

So, I ask you again, what are *you* playing for? There's power in asking yourself what you play for both in the short term and the long term. There's power in understanding what inspires you, why you get out of bed in the morning, why you do what you do. Once you understand what you're playing for, this can be the energy source that drives you forward to keep you focused on tough days. God knows that, as salespeople, staying focused and inspired can be the magical fuel that keeps our tanks full when they run low. Why not own what you want in your life and make it happen? Why not get really personal and clear about what you are playing for?

I'd like to tell you another story, about a teammate I coached. Before I started working with him, he put up pretty good numbers and, by all accounts, was a pretty good salesperson. But he wasn't consistent or focused, and I don't think he was clear about why he did what he did, why he had the job that he had, or where he wanted to go.

So, one day in our one-to-one sales meeting, instead of going through his activities, digging into his pipeline, and seeing what we could unstick or close, we put everything aside, and I asked him the same question I've been asking you.

"What are you playing for?"

After what was probably only minutes but which felt like a lot more to both of us, he finally answered.

"Karl, I want to change my life. I really want to marry my girlfriend, buy a nice house, and start a family. I want to give her all the things that she wants. I want to provide for us and give our kids all the things I never had. So, I guess that is what I am playing for…I am playing for my future life."

Now we were both clear on his why, and this clarity became very powerful. From that time on, I started each meeting by asking him how his plan and relationship were going, and if he was still fired up by the vision he had painted for me. The answer was always yes, and this motivation drove more and more of his focus. It was incredible to witness him raise his game through both Iceberg Selling and the clarity of what he was playing for. That December, he bought an engagement ring, and the following year he and his fiancée were married.

In what other profession can you reach for the sky like that? In a lot of other positions and career paths, they only have the framework of making a set amount of money a year. It's consistent, which some people like better, but in sales, we don't want those limits. And the impact we make is deeper than just money. As we become more successful, we create more and more stability for our team and those around us.

So, I want you to keep asking yourself, *What am I playing for?* What do you want in your life? What fills you up? How does your role as the master of your own destiny (what others might call "your role in sales") enable you to have that every day?

## It Begins and Ends with You

A lot of us have heard that you shouldn't take things personally. Forget what you have been told. I'm going to tell you to flip that around. If you are in sales, you need to take things personally.

In case you're having a "What in the what?" moment, I'll say that again.

Take sales personally.

In the following pages, I'm going to describe mindset shifts and best practices that will help you go from being a good salesperson to a great salesperson. But in the end, nobody is going to make those changes for you. I'm showing you a door, but you're the one who needs to open and walk through it.

If you're sitting here going, "I wish I could be more successful. I wish I could make more money," you can make that wish come true for yourself. You have the ability to change; you have the ability to pivot.

With Iceberg Selling, I'm going to give you one of the most powerful tools I've ever found to go from being a good salesperson to a great salesperson. And the best part is, it takes only a shift in attitude and mindset to see powerful results.

# ICEBERG SELLING GUIDE

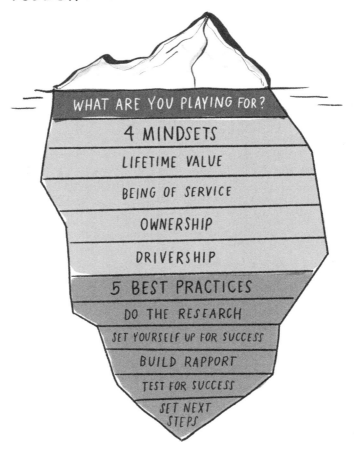

WHAT ARE YOU PLAYING FOR?

4 MINDSETS

LIFETIME VALUE

BEING OF SERVICE

OWNERSHIP

DRIVERSHIP

5 BEST PRACTICES

DO THE RESEARCH

SET YOURSELF UP FOR SUCCESS

BUILD RAPPORT

TEST FOR SUCCESS

SET NEXT STEPS

# Everything Is an Iceberg

Everything you see and everyone you meet is only showing you 10 percent of their story. Approach sales—and everything else—knowing 90 percent is below the surface.

- A lifetime-value mindset brings you much more value than looking only at the transaction in front of you.

- A being-of-service mindset helps you create value outside of the typical day-to-day sales role that most salespeople fall into.

- An ownership mindset gives you the power to author your own story and architect the experiences you want to create.

- A drivership mindset empowers you to create urgency, make things happen, and move opportunities forward with intentionality and greater success.

**Has your partner ever yelled at you about how you're** loading the dishwasher wrong? Did they seem a little more upset than they should be about something so basic? Chances are, there was something deeper than that going on, another reason they were frustrated with you. They just weren't saying it.

Have you ever seen a little kid have a full-on meltdown because someone told them to put socks on? It probably wasn't about the socks. It was probably because they were overtired, or didn't want to go home, or a combination of the zillions of reasons kids cry.

And, more to the point of this book, have you ever had a great call with a new customer only to have them ghost you? Chances are there were things going on with them you didn't know about, either. That's because, even in sales, there is always more to a situation than meets the eye.

That leads me to the number one rule I want you to get from reading this book.

Everything is an iceberg.

Icebergs that float out in the oceans come in all different shapes and sizes. Some are pointed, some are round, some flare out, and other ones go straight down. Some of them are huge, and some of them, if you blink, you'll miss. The one thing they have in common is that they are all 90 percent underwater.

And just because you have seen one iceberg doesn't mean you are an expert on every single one. To navigate an iceberg safely, you need to explore it, or you might end up crashing into it and sinking (even if you think you're the king of the world).

You know that your partner is annoyed with you, that the toddler is crying, and that a customer hasn't gotten back to you, but that's only 10 percent of what is actually going on in any given situation. Each one of those things are symptoms of something bigger. They're only the actions you see on the surface. There's always a lot more happening below that.

Keeping your partner happy with you is about more than doing the dishes their way. It's about truly understanding who they are, what fills them up and what wears that down. It's about seeing your partner in their entirety and meeting them there. If you want the toddler to stop crying, shouting at them to be quiet won't do the trick. But taking a moment to understand why your two-year-old is raging might be a good next step. When you spend the time investigating and getting curious about the root cause, the path forward often becomes clear.

It's no different with your customers. As a good salesperson, you know every customer is a little bit different. You don't assume one person or company needs the same thing as another. That leads to misreading a situation, getting ghosted, and losing sales. If you want to find out what's keeping a customer from responding to you, you need to understand what is really important to them. You need to be sure you showed them enough value and understanding in your last interactions and that you provided a clear and compelling path forward.

In the world of sales, one of the biggest and most frustrating risks is getting stuck in something I call the check-in zone. You've probably been there and know what I mean. It's that place where you think you created value, and you think things went well in your interactions, but the customer stops responding to you and you feel you have been ghosted.

So now you find yourself in that dreaded place…that place where all you feel you can do is check in. You observe yourself leaving voicemails or text messages or writing emails with empty lines like…

"Hey, do you have any questions? I'm just checking in."

"Just pinging you again to see if there's anything I can do for you."

"Do you need anything? Please reach back out if you'd like to talk further."

"Hey, I haven't heard from you in a while—are you breaking up with me?"

(Okay, that last one might not apply to your customers, but you get the picture.)

Getting stuck in the check-in zone feels horrible. Suddenly, we don't feel like we have any traction or any path forward. We have no idea why things have stalled, and we start to send more and more desperate messages. What is happening is we start to make the sales about ourselves and what we need, but we disguise it in language about helping them or answering their questions.

After all my years working in sales, I can tell you that in the check-in zone, it's super likely you've run into trouble because you looked only at the 10 percent of the customer's iceberg that is above the surface.

If you don't walk away from this book with anything else, there's one thing I want you to remember. To go from being a good salesperson to a great salesperson, you need to think about every person, every event, and every company you deal with as an iceberg. And to really keep out of trouble, you can't wait to do so until you've already run into it.

When you are first getting an understanding of what a customer wants from you, you are just seeing what is on the surface. Learn to look deeper and you find more ways to connect. Then you start to build stronger relationships. Navigating an ocean full of icebergs involves preparing the right way and moving forward with confidence.

Now, that doesn't mean icebergs are purposefully out to sink you, just like the people and situations you encounter every day aren't there to trip you up. They are just there, going about their iceberg business, and it is up to you to decide what to do with them. Do you want to pass them by? Do you want to stop to explore them? Or do you want to pretend they aren't there and risk wrecking everything?

No matter what you decide, you never know what's going on with an iceberg from one look. Lacking knowledge creates risk, whether you are steering a boat off the coast of Greenland or heading into a sales call.

With Iceberg Selling, you'll be at lower risk, and you'll be ghosted less and less. Your customers tell you they want to buy from you, and together you will chart next steps and get into mutual agreement on the path forward. As a bonus, the more you see everything as icebergs, the better you'll connect with other human beings. That's because when I say, "Everything is an iceberg," I mean *everything*. Your family, your friends, your colleagues, your customers, your favorite barista—all of them have entire stories that you will only know if you seek to understand them.

So, here are the first steps in how you can train yourself to be an Iceberg Seller. It starts with you tapping into four mindsets: a lifetime-value mindset, a being-of-service mindset, an ownership mindset, and a drivership mindset.

## The Lifetime-Value Mindset: Look Beyond the Deal

Sometimes salespeople get tunnel vision about closing sales. Okay, a little more than sometimes. Often salespeople get stuck obsessing over getting a deal signed, and that obsession reflects a transactional attitude and not the much more sustainable lifetime-value mindset.

Here is a story about a salesperson I know who got totally fixated on the deal. His name is Ethan, a salesperson at an events company called United Events.

I was running United Events' weekly sales meeting with a team of six salespeople, and it was Ethan's turn to speak.

"So, Ethan, do you have any deals that are stuck right now?" I asked him.

"Yeah, I do," he said. "I met this meeting planner about six months ago at a conference, and we totally hit it off. Her company was a perfect fit, and I think we could do a ton of events with them. About a month ago, she sent me an RFP for an upcoming event, so I answered it and created what I thought was a great proposal. I sent it to her about two weeks ago, and I haven't heard anything back. I've called, left voicemails, and sent emails. Now their event is coming up, and I don't know if we are doing it or not. I'm really frustrated."

The team started throwing out solutions for him, bringing up questions that he could ask and giving him advice on how to word his next outreach to her. It was all the same sort of awkward check-in zone outreach that salespeople seem to always do in these situations, the ones that make them look more and more desperate as they try to close the deal.

Finally, I stopped the conversation.

"Time-out," I said. "Ethan, do you care about winning this one RFP, or do you care about the lifetime relationship with this meeting planner and her company?"

He paused and then said, "The lifetime relationship with the meeting planner."

"Great," I said. "So, don't do anything right now that's going to jeopardize that. Do yourself and her a favor and don't keep checking in. What is done is done. Refocus on how you can be now to ensure you have opportunities later. Maybe this one will work out, but try not to get yourself all worked up. If you truly are after the relationship, then play for that, and you'll have much greater success in the long run."

Ethan's mindset wasn't serving him or the customer. In fact, it was putting his relationship with her at risk. Reaching out again and again about whether United Events was going to produce her upcoming event was making Ethan look a little desperate and was risking the original vision of the two companies working as partners on events over time. No matter how he wordsmithed his messages, his actions were all about being awarded the RFP. Ethan had gotten distracted from what would create value for the meeting planning company and how United Events could best support the customer. It has become all about closing the immediate deal.

That mindset was completely changing his behavior too. He needed to get out of his head and stop second-guessing himself. Not hearing back from the meeting planner was wreaking havoc on his confidence and causing him to make poor decisions that could affect the long-term potential of the account. This kind of change in perspective—away from the short term and toward the long term—is at the core of Iceberg Selling.

I want you to think about all the people you sell to and ask yourself how you look at the relationship with them. Is it about the lifetime or a short-term transaction? When considering the ones in the second category, take a step back. Instead of trying to force a deal, think about how you can create more value and build a relationship where they see you as worth working with in the future. There's a real cost to hyper-focusing on getting someone to sign on the dotted line only so you can make your monthly sales goal.

Even if a deal doesn't work out, even if you never end up working with a customer, working toward lifetime value over short-term deals can do wonders for your company's reputation.

In contrast, another events company, All-Productions AV, has a great track record with their customer relationships and a ton of lifetime value customers. At their core, they are a group of professionals who care about putting on great events. So they follow up with every lead who decides to work with someone else to produce their event. They also follow up with every lost deal a few days after the event they would have produced. They do this for a few reasons. Companies that put on events typically put on multiple events throughout the year, or at least they hold the same event every year. So, in a way, they are evergreen leads.

All-Productions AV also reaches out as a way to reflect the value of their brand, that they are always looking to support companies, their messages, and the outcomes they want to achieve from their events. By reaching out after an event, they are positioning their company as one that cares, full of people who are genuinely interested in the event host's success and believe in communication and collaboration. It also shows the customer that they play for the long-term relationship and not just the one-off opportunity.

Whenever they reach out to customers who ended up going with another event company, they get extremely positive responses that reflect the spirit of building valuable long-term relationships versus chasing deals. Here are a few of the real-life responses they have received.

*"I'm very impressed by the professionalism and comprehensiveness of the proposal and All-Productions AV's process compared to other event providers. Thank you for reaching back out and asking about our event."*

*"Your professionalism and dedication throughout the engagement were commendable. I genuinely hope that we will have an opportunity to work together in the future."*

*"All-Production AV's workflow, the proposal you provided, and the portfolio of offerings were the best, undoubtedly!"*

Consider what you are playing for in your interactions with customers. Is it the lifetime value or the immediate transaction? Depending on the impression you want to create, you can't lose sight of how your actions affect your relationships. Ask yourself whether you're forcing or manipulating a decision rather than creating value.

If you want to make a lasting, positive impression on your customers or even other people in your industry, taking on a lifetime-value mindset is the way to do it. And remember, when you're Iceberg Selling, it's not just about the value that having a long-term customer can bring to you. Even more, it's about the value you can bring to others.

## The Being-of-Service Mindset:
## Be a True Resource for Your Customer

When your sales approach is focused on others, you create value outside of the service you want to sell to them. Knowing what will be of service to someone involves looking deeper than the tip of the iceberg.

About six years ago, I worked with a company to develop their sales process and train their team. Four years later, they contacted me again. The market had changed, and they wanted me to look at their sales pipeline and the sales team's performance and see if I could find ways to create more success. As I started the engagement, I met their new director of marketing, Blake. I instantly liked Blake. He was smart, driven, and dedicated to making things happen. He also knew that success would compound if he could make sure sales and marketing were working well together.

So, I met with the company's three salespeople and reviewed the sales process. As I dug into the deals in different stages of their sales funnel, I found a lot of quick wins and strategized with the team to get the sales funnel moving again. It all worked, and the sales and marketing team could feel the energy and forward movement.

At the same time, I could see that Blake wanted more and that he was maxing out his current abilities. When I learned that the CEO wanted to add another salesperson and was about to ramp up a job posting, I did what comes naturally for many of us, and what I believe any of us would do if we realized we could create even more value for our customers. I reached out to my network, shared the job posting, and actively recruited a few salespeople I thought would be interested in the position. One of them got really excited, and I made an introduction.

Another one of my clients was about to hold a half-day marketing workshop, which I knew would create a ton of value for Blake. I called my client and told him about Blake, and he invited him to the workshop with a comp ticket as a professional courtesy to me.

I didn't need to do any of that. I could have stayed within the lanes of my assignment and been happy with the quick wins and the momentum of the team. Instead, I added value outside the engagement. I looked beyond the tip of the iceberg. As I learned more and more about what this client needed, I could create more and more value.

There's another dimension to this too. The salespeople I recommended that the company interview for the new job benefitted. So did my friend who was running the workshop that Blake attended. That's because being of service isn't a box you check when you're doing a job. It's a mindset, a way you approach everything in life.

We all know the phrase "you get what you give," but most people don't give just to get something out of it. Giving is worth more than that, and receiving things in return is never guaranteed. We give because we want to be of service to others.

For me, I feel good, I feel complete, I feel connected when I can support others. It's part of how I am wired, and in my experience, it's part of how most salespeople are wired.

If you're reading this book, you're probably wired to be a giver. You're playing for yourself, of course, but you're also looking to create value in the relationships that you have, both within your job and outside of it.

But maybe you haven't really figured out how to go the extra mile with your customers. My invitation to everyone I coach, to the rooms of people I speak to during conferences is to give this spirit of service a try—even if it's for only a moment. Think of a customer you know, or a colleague, friend, or family member, and then look at them as an iceberg. What do you know about them already, and what's underneath that? What do they want to accomplish right now? What are they going through? And what is something you could do for them to make a difference in their life right now?

If you're having a hard time figuring out how to get inside of another person's world, imagine that some kind of *Freaky Friday* thing just happened to you and one of your good customers. Suddenly you're in their shoes. Ask yourself what your world is like right now. What do you know about your new self, personally? What's it like for you at work? Is it stressful? Is there a major initiative or deliverable that is due? Is there a project or a goal that is keeping you up at night? Why did you reach out to, well, the real you in the first place? Why are you a current customer or a company thinking about being a customer? Then think about what you want from someone, how that person could positively affect your world. Back in your own life, in your own shoes, you can deliver that to your customer.

Ethan at United Events, for example, could share what he has seen firsthand that delights audiences. He could provide inspirational photos of past events his company has produced, offer a list of favorite event venues, or better yet, offer to visit these venues with his customer. He could even invite his customer to be a guest at one of his (other) upcoming events so that she could witness his brand firsthand.

Other ideas that work for any field include asking your customer if they would like to meet for a coffee to talk shop and explore how your two companies could partner together in the future. You could introduce them to clients you've worked with before on similar projects so they can compare notes and share experience and ideas. Even if it just expands their network, you're still giving them something that enriches them.

Whatever you think up, it's the intent that you put behind it that creates the real value. By following the being-of-service mindset and making it a habit, you can't help but see more of what is going on with the people around you. You will see more of the iceberg, and this in turn will create more opportunities to be of service as well as create more and more value.

## Ownership Mindset: Take Control of Your Reality

Did you know that you can take control of a situation and influence the outcome? Well, you can. It's so obvious that lots of people can't see it. And it's super true in the world of sales.

Many people don't realize how much power and control they can have over their own experiences. They think they can't act until someone gives them permission. You might even witness this in your sales organization—salespeople waiting to act until their sales manager tells them what to do. This goes against one of the most powerful reasons people decide to get into sales. Remember when I asked you to determine what you were playing for? Hopefully when you thought about why you were in sales you felt charged up and in control of your own destiny. If that's the case, why are any of us waiting for others to say it's okay?

Here's the good news. You've got a job to do, and you don't have to wait for permission to get into action. You are the author of your own story. You are the architect of your own experiences and the experiences you want to create for your customer and the accounts you manage.

Some of you might not fully believe me. Maybe there is a voice in your head saying, *I wish that were true.* It *is* true. You're in sales. You are a professional who was hired to make things happen. You're independent, smart, driven, and motivated. This is why it's so important to get connected with what you want and where you want to go, why it's so important to claim what you are playing for. It's the fuel of confidence and action.

No one other than you is standing in your way of owning your reality. Believe it and act on it, because the ownership mindset might be the biggest and most important mindset in sales.

So, what exactly is an ownership mindset? It's taking all the responsibility for something. One hundred percent. In sales, this means you get to decide how you want to show up for a new customer and how you want to manage an account. It means that you are a leader who decides how to design an experience then makes it happen.

The ownership mindset also applies to how you want to shape your own future. If there is something that will shape the future you want for yourself, you obsess over it and make it happen. Need more skills? Then advocate for yourself and get more education and training. Want to be in the President's Club? Then get motivated, create a plan, and work the plan until you achieve that.

With an ownership mindset, you get to decide what you want to do and how you want to be in any situation. An ownership mindset is not letting someone else decide what you do next. It's about owning what you think is the right next move and not giving up until you make it happen.

Making the ownership mindset shift—from waiting for permission to saying, "Wait a minute, I really am in control"—can totally change the game. It can totally change your life. This simple belief empowers you to do a lot more with what you have, leading to big wins and moving you from being a good salesperson to a great one.

Let me tell you about Jessica. Jessica lives in Denver and sells for a professional services company. She is responsible for opening new accounts as well as for retaining, managing, and growing the accounts she brings in. The company has a distributed team with clients all over North America. While she is in Colorado, the corporate offices are in Kansas City. I had been coaching Jessica for a few months, and the company had tagged her as a rising star on the sales team for her ability to open new accounts and effectively represent the company.

One day the CEO called and asked her to take over an account he had recently brought into the company through his personal network. It was a big deal for Jessica, and it was also a big deal for the CEO to let go of the account.

The CEO knew the customers at this account very well, and he told Jessica, "I think you can grow this account and turn it into one of your top five accounts." Jessica was almost bouncing off the walls when she told me all of this in our coaching session.

Over the next month, every time I met with Jessica, I would ask her what was going on with this new account. Week after week, she would give me answers like "I reached out to them with an email but haven't heard back," and, "I am not sure I know what the CEO wants me to do with this account," and, "I think it's going well, but I'm not really sure."

I don't think Jessica ever realized that she had the agency to fully own this account, to be the individual fully responsible for its success and growth.

After several weeks of those answers and a general feeling that Jessica wasn't making things happen with this account, I finally asked her, "Can I tell you why the CEO gave you this account and what he expected you to do with it?"

Jessica said, "Yes, please! Because I am feeling really lost about what to do next."

This is what I told her and what I would tell any salesperson in a similar scenario:

"If you want to grow this account, then you need to take the actions to really own it."

I told her to prioritize getting to know everything and everyone involved with the account. She should manage up and get on the CEO's calendar to learn everything he knows about it, why he thinks it could be a top five account, and any advice he'd have for her. Then she should do everything she could to connect with the customer to learn about them, their company, their current state, and their desired future state.

"Schedule a trip to Kansas City to meet with them, do your homework ahead of the trip, and bring ideas you think will both resonate and generate value for them. Commit to understanding everything you can about this new account and to being of service to them, think bigger than what they buy from you, and focus on building a high-value, ongoing partnership. Prioritize your time to support this account and step into a proactive role where you are thinking about how you can bring them value throughout the year…and then do it."

## Drivership Mindset:
## Make Things Happen with Greater Success

Feeling urgency. Being proactive. Deciding you are the driver and not the passenger. This is what the drivership mindset is all about—making things happen and not waiting for them to happen to you.

Let's say a new customer comes into your sales pipeline. You review the background on the customer, and the customer is perfect in every way you can imagine. They have the budget, the authority, and the need, and they want to move quickly. So, what are you going to do about it? If it's five when you get the assignment and you are about to leave for the day, are you going to follow up in the morning? Or are you going to reach out right away?

Great salespeople are drivers, plain and simple. They are the ones in constant motion, moving from one action to the next. We can see this in how they approach situations, solve problems, and overcome challenges.

A new opportunity comes in. They are on it.

A customer reaches out with a question. They respond right away.

They have an idea to generate more sales. They get intentional, and they get to work.

Some salespeople seem to be more passenger than driver. They wait for their sales manager to tell them what to do; they wait for the phone to ring or the next email request from their customers. When it comes to closing deals in their pipeline, they usually have an excuse for why they shouldn't reach out to drive things forward. These salespeople say things like:

"Oh, I didn't know I was supposed to do that."

"Well, the client didn't give me that information."

"I am still waiting for them to call me back."

"I don't want to bug anybody."

Great salespeople don't say things like that. Instead of giving up responsibility, I want you to be the driver who is already planning the next step, and the step after that, and the step after that. Be the salesperson who knows where they want to go and guides the customer there.

No one is going to do your work for you. No one is going to swoop in and magically make you a success. Success is up to you, and with a drivership mindset, you can make it happen.

Some salespeople resist a drivership mindset out of a fear of being too aggressive, too pushy, or too salesy. To that, I say, if you're truly creating value, if you truly can help your customer with their problems, if you truly can create a better reality for your customer, then you have the responsibility to take control and guide your customer forward.

Let's say you are a recruiter who specializes in placing nurses at hospitals. Customers come to you to staff their hospitals so that they can continue to serve patients and save lives. Now let's imagine a rural hospital calls you to help them find an emergency room nurse. They are in dire need. Their current staff is overworked, and they are the primary medical facility for the community. You take the assignment, and your point of contact tells you they are about to go on vacation. Then fortune smiles on you and you find an amazing candidate who is interested in the position and open to moving. What do you do?

What do you think would bring more value to the hospital: waiting to contact your customer when they come back from vacation or calling them right away?

If you have a drivership mindset, you call them now and move your candidate forward as fast as you can, for both your customer's and the candidate's benefit. And guess what—most likely both your customer and the candidate will thank you for your urgency and for taking the reins and moving things forward. And so will the community and the staff at the hospital.

If you truly have something of value, put it forward.

Act decisively. Act quickly. Make things happen.

## Mindset Shifts Help You See Below the Surface

With Iceberg Selling, you will raise your game. You will increase your own performance, have more confidence, communicate more effectively, and close more business. You will also feel more connected to your customers and be seen as a partner in their success.

A lifetime-value mindset, being-of-service mindset, and ownership and drivership mindsets are the baseline you need to go from a good salesperson to a great one. They're the landmarks you'll use as you navigate what I'm about to share with you. Plus, if you're able to make even the smallest of the mindset changes or start using a few of the best practices I'm going to give you in this book, you will see results fast.

You will see your life change. You will achieve what you're playing for. So, let's dive in.

# Best Practice #1—
# Do the Research

Before you even speak with the customer, identify the 10 percent of their story that is visible. Then go deeper.

- Identify what's on the surface. If you don't know the basics, you're missing out on the lowest-hanging fruit.

- Invest the time to find what isn't obvious. It's worth it, but most people don't bother.

- Do a deep dive into all the available information. The more you learn, the better your odds of success.

Remember, only 10 percent of an iceberg is visible, so 90 percent is below the surface. In sales, this is often the same. When we come across an opportunity, we often only see 10 percent of what is really going on. So, if 90 percent of information you need to know from a customer is hidden, how do you discover what is below?

First, you need to learn how to get great at understanding that hidden 90 percent, including everything you can find out before you even speak with the customer. You are surrounded by icebergs, and seeing them for what they are will add dimensions to your life and work that you never even thought of. Let's go through an example of how thinking more deeply can make you more successful.

Imagine you are planning a surprise eightieth birthday party for your dad. You love the guy—after all, he is your dad—and you want to do something special for him. You know about the things that every birthday party needs—that 10 percent that you can rattle off without even thinking about it. Any good birthday party needs a cake, a list of people to invite, probably balloons, a place to have the party, and so on.

But knowing the deeper details is going to take the party from good to great, and probably keep it from crashing and sinking. You don't get just any cake. You get your dad's *favorite* cake. You invite the people who are important to him, and then you take their needs into account too. What might they need to make it super easy to say yes to the invitation and help you celebrate your father?

I'm for real here. Think about the eighty-year-olds you know. Here's a pop quiz to help us plan.

Question: Should the party be during the day or go late into the night?

Answer: Older folks don't see well at night. Walking in the dark or even driving a car at night might be a hard pass for some of your dad's friends. Go with daytime.

Question: What about food? Should you be prepared for special considerations?

Answer: Absolutely, if you want to make the party inviting for your dad's friends and show that you care about creating a great experience for them (and if you want to make sure they tell your father how great of a child you are!).

I think you get the idea. Looking at everything as an iceberg is not only smart, but it creates advantage and increases your odds of success.

So, where do we start? At the easiest and most obvious place: all the above-the-surface information. That might sound basic, but doing everything that's visible and then going the extra mile is something that not a lot of salespeople take the time to do. You will find that doing even a small amount of preparation will put you at a better advantage than not doing anything at all. Very likely, it'll give you an immediate edge over your competitors too.

## Identify What's on the Surface

Have you ever heard the phrase "chance favors the prepared"? This is what we are talking about: increasing your chance of winning by the preparation you do.

When you're ready to explore an iceberg, start with the 10 percent you can see. If you aren't gathering all the surface-level information about the customer and the company you're working with, you're putting yourself on a collision course with the iceberg.

I used to run a digital agency where we built websites. It was pretty prestigious and won a lot of awards. Many people wanted to work there, so we interviewed lots of candidates as our success fueled our growth.

Within the first five minutes of every interview, I would ask, "When you looked at the portfolio section on our website, which projects did you like the best?"

I would know instantly whether they had done any research. The ones who could tell me their favorites and share with me the details of why had obviously done the work and wanted to be there. If they couldn't, the interview would go down the fast track and end early. These candidates were always a hard pass, because how they represented themselves in an interview was a clue to how they'd represent my company.

If you don't look for the clues, it's just poor form. If a sports team doesn't put their effort into training and watching the game tapes of their competitors and learning about the opposing team's strengths and weaknesses, they are certainly not increasing their odds of winning.

Salespeople need to make their own pre-meeting preparations as well or risk losing against themselves. You have to do the pre-work, and you have to put in the effort. Nothing is promised. Hard work creates success.

It's never been easier to find out about a person and their work. There is checking whatever social media feeds they have made public, including their LinkedIn. You can get information about how long they've worked somewhere, where they have worked before, and what positions they have held.

Pre-work starts with figuring out what the customer most likely already knows about your company and your offering and what they most likely still need to learn. Understand what makes your offering valuable and how you stack up against the competition. It's also about learning about your customers, both the person you'll be talking to and the company they represent. What is the individual's job title and responsibilities? What most likely is important to them? What has their career been like? From a company perspective, identify the company's vision, mission, core values, culture, offerings, and core customers. Ask yourself if they seem like a great fit or not. Ultimately, learn what you can, be curious, get intentional, and thoroughly prepare yourself for each meeting you have.

One of my clients is a boutique coffee roaster who also has a retail coffee shop. This client originally came to me as a referral, but before we even talked about working together, I used everything that was in front of me to find out more about them. That started with asking the person who referred me a ton of questions, researching the founder on LinkedIn, and carefully reading about their company values, origin story, vision, and product lines on their website and social accounts. Then, because their retail store was relatively close to where I live, I headed over one morning for a visit. I ordered a cappuccino (which was quite good, by the way), looked at the variety of their roasted coffee offerings, bought a bag of coffee beans, and chatted up the barista about what it was like to work there. It was a fun mystery shopping experience, but also a really great way for me to immerse myself in their brand. A few days later, when I had a sales call with the owner, I had firsthand experience of his company and their coffee.

All that information was all easily available; it simply required a little effort to find.

And that is the lesson here. Put in the time, do the work, and be a professional. Set yourself up to win and increase your odds of success. It's as easy as it sounds. It requires only intention and commitment to being the best you can be. Remember, success is yours if you own it.

## Invest the Time

You may also have heard the quote "luck is where preparation meets opportunity." In a lot of ways, that's true. If you have a drivership mindset, you make your own luck by investing your time and energy into learning as much as you can. Not doing your research is basically leaving money on the table. It might also lead you into situations that may look unlucky (while, really, they're just demonstrating your lack of preparation).

I'm going to tell you a story about something I did early in my career. It's not something I'm proud of, and at the end, I bet you'll say, "Wow, I really don't want to be that guy." But hopefully, me telling you about it will save you from going through something similar.

When I was twenty-one years old, I was working in the financial industry at a firm with a bullpen of financial advisors. When a financial advisor left, the sales manager would want to protect that book of business and make sure it stayed within the firm. They would give all the highest-performing, best accounts to the remaining top salespeople. If you were a more junior advisor who hadn't been there for very long, you would be lucky to get anything, and if you did, it was most likely an inactive account, where the customer hadn't been in contact with the financial advisor for years.

At face value, these accounts felt more like obligations than gifts, but it could also be a chance to re-engage an old customer and make a strong impression with your higher-ups. When one of those old accounts landed on my desk, that was exactly what I wanted to do.

I did what I thought was enough research: flipping through the information file that I had been given. I looked at the securities that this person owned and saw they had some stock that had gone up about 30 percent over the past few months. I couldn't believe my luck. To me, that meant this person was making money with our firm and the financial advisor before me must have done something that was really of value. This was my chance to turn an already pretty good situation into something great.

"Hi, there," I said, super excited, when I called the account owner. "My name is Karl Becker, and I am a financial advisor at DWR, and I was assigned your account. Do you have a minute, by chance?"

"Sure," she said.

"So, I bet you're feeling pretty good. I see you own some Atari. It's gone up about 30 percent over the last few months!"

That was when I found out I wasn't as lucky as I thought. In fact, I had really stepped in it. What I didn't realize was she had been in that account for over ten years. When she had bought that stock...well, it was a $20,000 investment, and now it was only worth $5,000. As of the day I called her, she had lost $15,000 overall. That 30 percent improvement, while representing some nice movement, was doing little to recoup the huge loss she had in the position.

I hadn't done enough preparation after all. Not by a long shot.

There were things I could have done to avoid that situation. For starters, I could have looked at the overall history of her investment rather than just the past few months. I even could have asked her a simple question about how her experience had been at the firm so far rather than taking off at full throttle. If I had spent the time getting to know the situation, it wouldn't have backfired so badly. I wouldn't have crashed into an iceberg I hadn't even bothered to look at.

To this day, I don't remember exactly what she said in reply, but I know it certainly wasn't positive. What I do remember, and still feel, is her unpleasant, frustrated, and condescending tone.

I had made the most junior mistake out there, and I felt like a fool. Even worse, I knew that in our weekly sales meeting, I would have to report what happened to my sales manager. Needless to say, I learned a huge, uncomfortable lesson on the importance of preparation.

To be fair to myself, I was twenty-one years old. Of course I was going to make a junior mistake. I didn't know what I didn't know. But here, thirty years later, it is still burned into my brain. I never want to feel the way I felt on the phone with her or reporting back in a sales meeting again. And I don't want you to feel that way either.

Here's what I recommend you do to avoid an embarrassing situation like this when you are preparing to reach out to someone. Prioritize looking at not just the data that's available online but all of your company's internal data. Is there anything about the customer in the CRM? Has someone from your company contacted them before? Are there any subjects, conversations, or questions that could end up sinking your ship? Try to spend as much time as you can to see as much of the iceberg as you can through any clues that you can pick up. And I mean *any* clues.

## Do a Deep Dive

There's one quality that plays into every single one of the best practices I'm teaching you.

Curiosity.

At the beginning of every relationship you have or project you take on, you don't know what you don't know. Asking questions is your biggest key to seeing the shape and depth of the iceberg. You are going to hold on to your curiosity from when you first engage with a customer, through your calls and interactions with them, all the way through the sale and beyond.

The more curious you are and the more you discover, the better odds you have of a successful relationship and, ultimately, a sale. So, use your imagination and live in a place of wonder as you explore all the parts of the iceberg even before speaking with the customer. If you stay in that state of curiosity, you're more likely to notice key parts of the iceberg that will be important as you navigate it later.

And it's not just facts about the services or products that the customer needs. It's not just about what they make, who's who, or how long they've been in business. It's not just dry trivia. It's the deeper questions about what they value and what's going on in their world, where they are now, and where they want to be.

Going the extra mile to learn what makes your customer click sets you apart from other salespeople. You're showing a commitment to learning and an interest in building a relationship even before you know whether you'll work together.

Several years ago, I had a goal to create a partnership between the company where I was working and a major retailer. We had a product that would work in tandem with theirs, creating a sort of brand within a brand. The retailer was a pretty big deal. At the time, it had about five hundred stores around the world, including one at my local mall.

It was a long shot to go after such a big fish, but I decided to lean in and learn more about the brand. I went to the nearby store a lot, so I could really understand the experience the company wanted to create. Then, I found out that the CEO had a book. I wanted to learn everything I could about her, so I read it. Since they were a publicly traded company, I also listened to recordings of their investor calls. In short, I made it my mission to learn everything about how they did business, what they stood for, their mission and values, and what drove the CEO to make the decisions that she made.

And by caring enough to read her book, I found that she had included her email address–her *direct* email address—at the end of it. I had the ticket in my hand that would help me get in touch with her, once I was prepared.

Finally, I'd done enough research that I was ready for the pitch. I was going to call her after five o'clock using the company's phone system. If she picked up, she probably wouldn't be interrupted and I would probably be able to talk to her. If she didn't pick up, I would leave a voicemail and then follow up using the direct email that I'd gotten from the back of her book.

I practiced what I was going to say. I practiced a lot. I wanted to come across as a real person with a real idea. I wanted to show up authentically and honestly and deliver my message with enthusiasm. And that's what I did.

When I did indeed get her voicemail, because I had done so much pre-work, I could let myself be unscripted, even a little rambling. After I introduced myself and told her I had a really fun idea I wanted to tell her about, I let her know I was going to send her an email. She was welcome to respond if she was interested, and even if it didn't end up going anywhere, I was looking forward to speaking with her and that my kids and I were huge fans of the brand.

When I got off the phone, my wife was standing at the top of the stairs, looking at me like I was out of my mind.

"Did you just leave that voicemail?"

She had heard me on calls for twenty years, and she was taken aback by how rambling and unscripted I had sounded as she eavesdropped.

I smiled and nodded. "I wanted her to hear my excitement and know that I was real and that it was important for me to share something I was passionate about."

After all the research and pre-work I'd done, I had confidence that that would be the right approach for this person. It turned out I was right. The CEO emailed me back later that night and even sent me a LinkedIn invite to connect. From there, we ended up getting an appointment on the books. In fact, she was heading to Denver to speak at a conference in the coming month, and we would end up meeting in person.

As I said in the previous chapter, not every iceberg is the same. By diving deeper and exploring more thoroughly than your competitors, you can get a good idea of each of their unique shapes. In this case, my intentionality, curiosity, and research had earned the attention of someone I was eager to work with.

## You Never Know What You'll Find

Opening yourself up to Iceberg Selling will change you forever. Maybe you won't find the clues that guarantee success every time you're curious, but you will dramatically raise your game. Your interest in learning more and more about another person's world will create connection, rapport, and trust. This will provide you with knowledge of what is important to them.

And from this knowledge, you will be able to bring forward ideas that support them as they move from where they are now to where they want to be.

# Best Practice #2—
# Set Yourself Up for Success

Chart the course you want to take, communicate your plan to your customer, then stay fully engaged with them.

- Architect your meeting. Decide what outcome you are playing for and create an experience that achieves it.

- Tell the customer where you are taking them. Clearly communicate the agenda or format for your meeting and then get their buy-in.

- Stay present for your customer, showing that they are the most important thing to you.

**If you have a drivership mindset in your first meeting** with a customer, you can make a much more effective impression. Completing thorough research lets you architect an experience that will make them want to spend more time with you. And if you really want a meeting to go well, go the extra mile to make the customer comfortable. They'll be much more enthusiastic about helping you explore more of their iceberg.

Careful meeting preparation also allows you to build in pivot points depending on what you learn about the customer and their needs. Those pivot points will be important later when you start exploring solutions.

Remember, your job is to be the driver and to craft a high-value meeting. You need to have the immediate next step ready, as well as ideas and strategies for future steps that will lead you and the customer to their desired state.

## Architect Your Meeting

Being a salesperson is like constantly interviewing for a job—and the interview starts whenever the customer says it does. Whenever I interview someone for a job, I try to watch the parking lot while I wait for them to show up. Often, a car will pull up and madly circle the lot, trying to find the right building. Ultimately, they find it and park, get out of the car, and start walking to the building. Sometimes, they'll run back to get something out of their car like their phone or résumé. Happens all the time.

Here is the uncomfortable truth: the interview starts as soon as I see that person pull into the parking lot. People can see you not just when you're ready for them to, but the moment you come into their view. And anything that distracts them from your offering doesn't reflect well on you.

People doing business with you want to be confident that you know what you're doing. A well-designed meeting communicates a lot. It sets the stage of what it is like to work with you, what is to come. And you want that stage to show that you are intentional, focused, and deliberate. That you respect their time and yours. Simply put, that you play good ball.

In the last chapter, I told you about how I got an appointment with the CEO of a major retailer. She had plans to come to Denver, and we were going to meet for lunch then travel to one of her stores to continue our conversation. I was going to knock this meeting out of the park, but that meant I wanted everything to be planned down to the smallest detail. There would be no surprises and no awkwardness because something didn't go the way I wanted. Not if I could help it.

Once I had made my detailed plan about how the meeting would go, I went for a practice run the day before. At the time, I had a soft-top Jeep Wrangler. It was a fun car to drive, but it was not the ideal vehicle to chauffeur a CEO of a Fortune 500 company around in. So, I called in a favor and borrowed a friend's car that felt a little more grown-up. I practiced driving to the CEO's hotel in downtown Denver, making sure there weren't any road closures and noting how long the ride would take. I found out what the parking situation was, and then went into the restaurant to get a feel for what it was like and whether it was quiet enough for a successful meeting. I looked at the menu, so I could plan what to get and not let anything distract me from the CEO.

Then, I did the same thing with the drive from downtown Denver to the mall where her store was. Again, I timed the trip and made a plan for parking. I went into the shop to see who would be working the next day and to let the staff know they would be getting a visit from the CEO.

All my intentionality paid off. The next day, there were no unexpected risk points. Even better, when I dropped the CEO back off at the hotel, she told me what a great meeting it was and that she wanted to do a pilot program for what I'd pitched to her.

Doing my research by reading her book, visiting her stores, and learning everything I could about the company had earned me her attention. Drawing a meticulous and practiced plan for how our meeting would go had set a thorough course for success. I had architected each step from beginning to end, and I knew exactly where I was going and how to get there. Everything was ready before she even arrived in Denver or I had walked into the hotel lobby.

Yes, I know this is a lot. But remember, you are on a path to go from good to great, a journey to make sure you achieve what you are playing for. I can guarantee most of your competitors won't dedicate this kind of time and intention. At best, most of them will do the bare minimum—a little research, a little planning—and then move on with the rest of their day.

Sure, they'll follow all the little rules that we've all been taught: show up early to an appointment, make sure your tech is working, mind your appearance, remove distractions, look the part, and use a breath mint. But they're still just doing 10 percent of what they could do, shining a light on the tip of the iceberg without seeing what the other 90 percent might look like.

I'm inviting you to figure out how you can bring more of yourself than you have before to your customer. Making a detailed plan, showing your customer where you plan to go, then staying present with them every step of the way might be a little uncomfortable. You will have to be vulnerable and show some of what's below the surface of *you*. And yeah, you will definitely have to work harder. But by using all four mindsets—lifetime-value, being-of-service, ownership, and drivership—you will realize you can set the stage and guide the customer to see a path forward with you, your company, and your offering.

## Show Them Your Plans

Your customer doesn't schedule an initial meeting with you for you to immediately say, "Okay, are you ready to buy?" Making a customer want to go on a journey with you involves not only creating a safe environment but sharing your design for the meeting with them. As the salesperson, you are the facilitator of every meeting. You are the mapmaker and the person steering the ship. But your customer is part of this too, and they will want to know where you are headed and what path you are all going to take.

Telling your customer exactly how things are going to go from the beginning is more than just a courtesy. It also helps you stay on course at points in the meeting that might be more stressful, particularly at the end when you talk about your next steps. Their expectations will be set, and they will appreciate not getting any curveballs as much as you will.

Explaining your path forward during a call might look a little something like this:

"I would love to spend a couple of minutes learning what you're looking for, so I can know what you're trying to achieve, a little more about you and your company, and what a successful outcome might look like. After that, I'd like to share some ideas about how we might help. As we are learning about each other, I want to make sure I'm covering everything that might help me find the right solution for you. Then, after that, we'll probably check in to see if this seems like the right fit or not. If it is, then let's talk through what possible next steps might be like or how we could work together to create a solution that works for both of us. If we find we might not be a fit, I will tell you that too. Does that sound like a good direction for our meeting?"

There it is, completely laid out for them. No part of the meeting will be a surprise to either of you. When you are agreeing on your starting place and giving them an idea of how you'll reach your destination, you are also revealing the places where they can give input. Even if you are the main driver, they can help you safely navigate what may not have been on your radar.

I really like telling people upfront where I'm taking them in a meeting. Sometimes I tell them in a narrative, like in that example, or I use an agenda (especially if it isn't my first meeting with a customer). It helps me get more buy-in and proves that I'm there to cooperate and co-create with them. I want to work with them and not against them. There are no shadowy spots where they might be ambushed. It's not buyer versus seller. It's collaboration, not confrontation. Remember, this is about building relationships. You will bring your being-of-service mindset rather than a transactional one.

## Stay Present

For my meeting with the CEO of the retail company, I brought along a set of product samples. During our lunch, she looked at each of those items one by one—carefully and deliberately. As we sat at the restaurant table, she silently looked through the package I had worked weeks and weeks to develop. I could see her mind turning, but the silence and slowness was intense, and I had to work hard to stay present. But this was what I had prepared for; this was the start of the big game, and I needed to play my part. As I remember that day, it was a classic example of patience and sitting in what might seem like discomfort.

For most of us, it's excruciating to sit in stillness, waiting for our customer to say something. We want to talk, to break what we believe to be uncomfortable silence and share all our ideas and opinions. But trust me here: resist this urge to show up and throw up (I bet you know what I mean, but we'll talk about this more in the next chapter). Instead, stay present. In this scenario, I pretended the CEO was my grandmother, treating each sample like she was searching for a favorite piece of chocolate nestled in a box of assorted chocolates at Christmas time. And I don't know about you, but I'd never rush my grandmother while she picked out her favorite piece of chocolate. Patience and understanding were critical.

So, I sat there, peacefully in the moment, and let this CEO process what was in front of her. I needed to let her be immersed in the experience I had taken months to create and let the work speak for itself. But it wasn't easy. I was nervous, and my distractibility was kicking in like mad. But few things are more important than staying focused on a customer, especially in crucial moments like this.

When I started working as an independent consultant, I used an answering service to screen my calls. It felt professional, and I wanted to seem like I had a bigger team than just me.

One morning, as I was in the kitchen making breakfast, the phone rang. It was the answering service. I picked up, and the receptionist told me I had Sarah Johnson from Hewlett Packard on the phone. She wanted to talk about a possible project with me. A ton of thoughts flashed through my brain in an instant just as my two dogs decided to start play-fighting and rolling around on the kitchen floor.

I tried to stay calm. Hewlett Packard? A project? Okay... wow.

"Could you give me just a minute?" I asked the receptionist.

"My switchboard is lighting up..." she said.

"Okay, count to five and then put her through." With no time to spare, I grabbed a whole jar of dog treats, opened the double doors to the backyard, and launched all the treats out onto the deck.

Not skipping a beat, I picked up the phone and answered it like nothing was happening as my feral dogs darted outside for a surprise treat extravaganza. And lucky for me too, as the call ended up being an immensely valuable conversation with a great project and amazing client who is still friends with me today.

Staying present isn't always going to be that challenging, but even if you have all the time in the world to prepare, there's always going to be distractions you don't expect. You don't always get the big conference room with glass doors, great lighting, and a whiteboard.

Ideally, business development and networking meetings let you exist in a place where you can be fully present with each other. A conference room, if you set it up correctly, can be like your own private stage, a safe space where you are the star and nothing bad can happen to you. You can curate and design it to make the impact you want it to. It can be part of a grand design in the experience you want to create for your customers.

It might be a more common experience for you to meet in a busy office, over the phone, or on a video call. Meeting someone in person makes it easier to fully focus on them. You wouldn't want your attention wandering from someone sitting at a conference table with you. But ideally, people on a call with you should also feel like you are in the room together.

No matter where you are, turn off your phone or put it in do-not-disturb mode. Give your full attention to the person you're talking to. If you know of anything that might interrupt you or cause a distraction, warn them at the beginning.

Once, I brought a person in for a ninety-minute lunch meeting. It was mostly just a meet-and-greet to see if we could work well together. I hadn't done much preparation for it other than bringing in lunch. All the basics were there, but I hadn't made the plans that would help me manage the time effectively.

As we reached the end of the meeting, I had finally built enough rapport that the person started opening up in a big way. The problem was, I had a meeting right after ours, and suddenly, I was ready to latch on to any squirrel that ran by. Even though this person was finally giving me what I needed to connect with them, all I could think about was the possibility of being late for my next meeting. I was looking at my phone to see what time it was. I was looking up whenever I saw movement. I felt like I was about to turn into a pumpkin. It was awful to realize what I was doing with my body language.

This was a big opportunity, but now that we were talking about moving forward, I was getting derailed. All the hard work that I did started to dissolve because I could not stay present with this person. Part of the problem was I hadn't designed a tight enough agenda and I didn't let the person know when I would need to move on to my next meeting. If you think about what we've learned about a drivership mindset, I had unwittingly made myself a passenger at my own meeting. And this unintentional misstep was now generating a lot of risk and putting what could be a great partnership in jeopardy, all because of me and my actions.

Of course it's way better to avoid this situation in the first place than to catch yourself and realize you're in trouble. Careful planning, with extra intentionality, is your friend. But the fact is, there are many people in sales who also have trouble staying focused. I get it—especially in longer meetings, it's easy to get distracted. Maybe your phone lights up, somebody walks by and waves at you, or you start thinking about meeting up with your friends after work.

Managing fallout from that requires being honest and proactive. The best kind of preparation comes before the meeting even starts, but the second best is knowing what to do in situations where you let yourself get derailed. Call out what is going on, be authentic, and own your actions. If you're simply having a tough time focusing and being present, you need to call a time-out.

The key is honesty and transparency. When you realize that you're not present, you're having a tough time focusing, and you can't repeat back what the person just said, look at the person and say, "Hey, could you do me a favor and repeat the last thing you said? I'm sorry, something distracted me, but it's important for me to know what you have to say."

Even if you don't like silence, even if you struggle with staying engaged, planning and preparation will help you deal with situations like that. Putting the meeting together intentionally, having a plan to deal with your distractible mind, and learning to be vulnerable will show your customers respect and help you bring your best self forward.

## Icebergs, Right Ahead

The time has come. You know where you're going, and you've gotten your customer on board. When both of you know where you are headed, it makes it possible for you to work together to fully bring the icebergs you are navigating into view. A collaborative approach means a higher likelihood of arriving at your destination in one piece, having thrived rather than just survived.

With your environment curated and your course set, you'll have a much easier time finding out all the things you need to know to have a successful call that is of service to everyone. Because of the preparation you've done, and with your customer primed and ready to move forward, you can go deeper than you ever would have if you hadn't taken the time or made the effort. You're ready not to have a good call, but a great one.

# Best Practice #3—
# Build Rapport

Rapport is about understanding, communication, and connection. Learn what is important to your customer and their organization, to truly get into their world.

- Be authentic and invested in learning about who this person is and what is important to them.

- Get curious about your customer, their business, and their organization. Ask questions and listen fully without interrogating them.

- Focus on connecting with the customer rather than putting on a performance. There will be plenty of time to share your solutions once you know about the customer and what they are looking to achieve.

**We talk about building rapport all the time.**

You might find yourself in a conversation with your sales manager, and they ask you if you built rapport during your last sales call. Or if I were to ask you why you were good at sales, you might tell me that you are great at building relationships and rapport with your customers.

Everyone knows that it's important to "build rapport" when you're in sales. But what does that really mean? I'm not sure many people know. I think a lot of the time, people think of rapport as about being friendly and likeable, understanding only the 10 percent of the iceberg that they can see on the surface. They think it's just about making the other person like them, when rapport is really much more than that.

Rapport isn't just showing someone a friendly face or making them think you're a nice person. It's not about convincing someone you're trustworthy and they should work with you. It's about connecting with people on a deeper level and getting an understanding of what's below the surface of the problem that they're bringing to you.

If you stay focused on making people like you, you are not being authentic, and you're probably too focused on yourself to understand the shapes of their icebergs. You end up putting on a show or talking over them, keeping you separated from them when what you want to do is connect.

In the end, the same thing that keeps you from building true rapport keeps people from experiencing many of the best parts of life: fear. Being afraid of crashing into an iceberg actually makes it more likely that you will. Instead, focus on the plan you've made, the knowledge you have, the experiences you can bring to the conversation, and a better understanding of what your customers need from you. Getting into the customer's story and away from the worst-case scenarios running through your head will keep you from focusing on what you are afraid of and instead help you explore and navigate safely.

Remember, your goal is to learn what is important to your customer and their organization. You are truly looking to get into their world. If you're going to build rapport with somebody, make them feel understood. They need to walk away from the conversation thinking, *Wow, that person really gets me.*

## Be Authentic

When I was in my early twenties, I moved to Boston. I didn't know anybody and was kind of lonely, but I liked exploring the city and meeting new people. One day, I decided to check out the area around the capitol, then grab a beer at an iconic downtown bar.

I was at the counter bar with my pretzels and beer, and a woman around my age entered the bar and sat a few seats down from me. So, because I was pretty outgoing, I started a conversation.

"Hi, there," I said. "How's it going?"

She barely acknowledged me but gave me a slight smile and said, "Okay."

"So, do you work near here?"

Immediately, her walls went up. "Why would you want to know that?" she asked.

Whatever she thought my intentions were, it became obvious that I had made a bad impression. Whether she was simply having a bad day, whether she had perceived my question as creepy or invasive, or whatever the situation might have been, her response came from a place of defensiveness. The thing I took away from this (other than I had no game in my twenties) is that lots of people are defensive until you reveal a little about yourself too. I often wonder if I'd introduced myself as just having moved from Denver and still getting to know the area, whether I would have gotten a less defensive response.

The less a person knows about you and your company, the more their walls will be up. Remember—you are an iceberg too, and so is your company. That's where a lot of salespeople get nervous. They think that if they just get in, get the facts, and give their presentation, they'll get out of that call without having to open up and put themselves out there. But that kind of canned interaction is transactional. It makes you seem like you don't care about anything other than making a sale.

You want to show a customer that you're really interested in learning about them and focused on how you can find a solution that supports them. Authenticity means showing up as your genuine self, but it's also about showing true interest in the person you are talking to.

Let's play a game. It's a simple game. I want you to remember the last time you went to a really nice restaurant for a really nice meal. Can you see the building? The table? Can you feel the ambience? Do you remember what you had to eat? Or the waitstaff? Or do you just remember the overall experience? Regardless of the specifics, I bet you can remember how nice of a time you had. I bet you can remember the overall feeling.

This wasn't an accident. If you have strong positive emotions from the experience, you were part of a nicely curated dining experience. I am also going to bet that your experience was positive partly because of how the entire waitstaff showed up and interacted with you and your guests. In short, your experience probably wasn't just because the food was remarkable—it was because everything (the whole enchilada, if you will) was.

Restaurants know this, and great waitstaff know this too. So much of the experience is how your server shows up, whether they greet you warmly, make eye contact, read the situation, and work to be present and engaged with you. Great waitstaff can recognize if it's a business dinner and you are in charge. In this situation, they will most likely ask you how you want the evening to go. If you are on a romantic date, great waitstaff read that too and work hard to make sure you have privacy and feel taken care of. If you're an older couple who looks to be celebrating their anniversary, they are going to ask you about it. In fact, they might even ask if you want to take any special desserts home to your children. All of this is to say that great waitstaff are great salespeople. They see what is above the water and then use those clues to go deeper, to learn more, and to adjust to what their guests want.

At my last nice restaurant experience, my wife and I were looking to steal away and have a late dinner. We arrived at one of our favorite restaurants, and as we walked in, the host apologized that the kitchen was closing, but the bar was still open for cocktails. We said we understood about missing out on dinner, explaining that we were just trying to get away from the kids for a bit, that we loved their restaurant, and that we'd see them next time. One of the servers overheard us and stepped forward, telling the host and the two of us she'd check with the manager and the chef to see if they could keep the kitchen open for another fifteen minutes. We were surprised and appreciative of her kindness.

This server was showing up with a being-of-service mindset and was going above and beyond to welcome us. We wanted a nice meal and a relaxing experience together before we went home to our teenage sons, and she was ready to support us in that.

She returned with good news. "We can stay open a little longer for you." She smiled as she led us to a beautiful table next to a window. "I totally get it. I have kids too. It's so hard to get away with my husband sometimes. I am so glad you are here."

The rest of the night was amazing. We were treated like royalty, and the server would occasionally check in with us and engage us in conversation. Not too much, just right. It was obvious she enjoyed what she did and that it was important to her that we had a memorable experience. And it worked. I can still tell you the name of the restaurant, our wonderful server's name, what she looked like, how old she was, and her favorite movie (*This Is 40*). She shared enough of her iceberg to make us feel comfortable with her, and she made an effort to understand us rather than just take our order.

As salespeople, we've probably all been trained to be pleasant, show up engaged, ask the person we are meeting with how much time they have, and ask what they want to make sure they get out of our meeting. We make a little small talk and then run a good sales call. There's nothing wrong with that, but none of it is going to build real rapport. If all you do is go through the motions with this type of checkbox sales mechanism, it won't feel authentic. It won't feel like you really care or that you are engaged in their success. You won't seem curious or like it matters to you who they are and what their world is like. Under this scenario, you are leaving a ton of value on the table and creating a ton of risk. Most likely, you and the customer will feel unsatisfied with the meeting because you didn't make a real connection.

Here's an example of when I was put off as a customer for this very reason. I had started a new company where we rented out cars, and I was evaluating different software platforms to enable direct bookings, manage our fleet, handle all the accounting functions, and fulfill all those other administrative parts of the business. After doing my research, I found a platform that I was pretty sure was perfect for us.

When I got on the sales call for the demo, I was amazed at how canned everything was. From a transactional point of view, the salesperson did everything right. He showed up on time. He had looked at our website. He was polite. He asked a couple questions about me, but nothing so deep that it would derail the presentation or take time away from him showing me the software's features. It was obvious he had formal sales training, but it was mechanical and didn't build rapport. It seemed like he was reading everything from a standardized call script with a checkbox next to each stage of the call, and he wanted to check "small talk" off that list as quickly as possible.

"Oh, you live in Colorado? I've heard the mountains are beautiful there. Anyway, let's jump into the demo and make sure we cover what you want to learn."

Every kind of token attempt to "connect" was surface level. I could tell that as I answered his canned questions. It felt like he was waiting for me to stop talking so he could move to the next stage and then the following stage of his demo. He didn't spend the time to really get to know why I was on that call and what we were looking to achieve. He didn't understand our iceberg at all, and he didn't remotely put effort into trying to do so.

## Be Curious

When you ask someone about themselves and you act like the guy who gave me that software demo, it can be super alienating. Imagine you asked a customer how they were doing, and they answered by telling you they'd had a stressful week. They went on to explain that their mother was in the hospital, their spouse was traveling on business, and they were having challenges with daycare.

Would you say, "Wow, that sounds really intense. I am sorry to hear that. By the way, did you see the agenda I sent over for our call?"

I sure hope you wouldn't! That's not great (and it isn't good either).

I'd like you to consider that when you're learning about someone's professional challenges, it can be just as personal a conversation as them telling you about their emotionally difficult and stressful week. Think of all the reasons why a company might be looking for your solutions. Depending on what you sell, this could be major stuff. Maybe your solution solves a real problem that is critical to their business, and sharing all their issues with you feels a little scary because it shows you that their company has problems. As your customer reveals more and more, you might learn that their job is on the line, their company has some real financial challenges, they are losing market share, and they are having a tough time with employee retention. Whatever it is, it can be hard for a customer to start sharing with you the truth of what is really going on.

That's why you being authentically curious is going to make your customer feel comfortable and more likely to trust you and share what is really going on beneath the surface of their iceberg.

And as I've said before, you never know what you'll find when more of that iceberg comes into view.

Curiosity isn't just about taking out your list of discovery questions and going through it like a robot. Bring in that curiosity you had when you started preparing for this meeting. This is the point where you're really exploring the iceberg. You're trying to understand as much about it as you can. Why are they, the individual, from this company, talking to you today? What's going on at their company? What do they want the outcome of this meeting to be? What is the desired state they are hoping to reach, the problems they are looking to solve?

It comes back to the being-of-service mindset and the lifetime-value mindset. Stay focused on finding out what is valuable for the customer. Even if they say no to an initial sale, being of service provides you both with long-term benefits, and you'll only know how you can help them if you're curious to learn about what they need.

That said, do remember that you need to be careful about how you ask questions. Have you ever heard the old sales advice "whoever asks the most questions wins"? It's advice that you should take with a heavy dose of salt. If you're focused only on asking your long list of questions, you could come across as a newspaper reporter who is only there to take their story, or even a police officer who is interrogating them for a crime.

The best talk show hosts, people who build the best rapport and draw out the most fascinating stories from their guests, don't sound like they're reading off a list of questions. They sound like they're having a conversation with a friend, and they learn a lot more about the person they're talking to that way. That's the experience you want to create with your customers.

Not being curious can also cut off conversations before they even get going. One story that sticks out for me is an afternoon that I spent with my wife when we were both young, working, and had no kids. It was Saturday, and as we drove through town, we spotted a car dealer's lot with a light-blue Volkswagen Bug convertible out front.

My wife immediately commented on it. The convertible's carefree feel and the smart placement on the lot was working its charm.

I smiled. It was a cute car. It looked fun. And I could easily envision her driving it around town the rest of the summer.

"Do you want to drive it?" I asked.

"I'm not buying that car," she said before I could even bring up the possibility.

"Right, but do you want to just drive it? A test-drive?"

I knew she did, and I am pretty sure she knew that if she really liked it, we'd buy it.

So, I asked again, but this time made it more of a statement. "Let's go check it out and take it for a spin... What do you think?"

She agreed, and we pulled into the lot. We got out of the car and casually strolled over to the car holding hands and looking starry-eyed. Within seconds, a younger sales guy came out of the dealership and warmly welcomed us. We told him we wanted to test-drive the Bug.

"Are you going to buy it today?" he asked.

"Probably not," I said.

"Well, then, why would I let you test-drive it?" he said.

And that was that. Conversation over. The whole thing was a little weird to us, especially to me as a salesperson. The lot was empty, it wasn't a busy day, and we were just the right type of people to buy a fun convertible—a couple in our thirties with no kids and dreamy expressions. There were plenty of opportunities for that salesperson to connect with us, to ask us why we wanted to drive it. To confirm it would be for my wife and for us to have fun. If we didn't want that car that day, maybe we would change our minds later. Maybe if we needed a car in the future, we would think of going to that lot first because we'd had a good experience with that salesperson. But he was thinking in a more transactional way and wasn't interested in having a conversation that he wasn't sure would end in a sale. He had no curiosity. He wasn't Iceberg Selling.

This is kind of a funny story, but without curiosity, you can hit a dead end just as fast as that car salesperson did. If you aren't curious, you miss not only the chance to sell but the chance to build relationships.

Even really smart salespeople can get transactional tunnel vision. They think they're being of service by asking over and over what someone needs: "Hi, I am calling to check in again. Let me know if there is anything you need."

That's mailing it in. It's not effective, and way too many salespeople take this approach, thinking it shows they are there for their customers.

Just asking whether someone wants to buy your product or service without fully understanding more about them, their company, and their situation isn't of service. It's not going to help you build relationships. You may even make people want to avoid you.

So, remember, when you're building rapport, communicate in a way that is relevant and valuable to the customer. During your conversation, spend about 90 percent of the time discovering who they are, what is important to them, and what problems they have that you might be able to solve. Maybe you won't hit every single thing on your agenda, but if you get them to talk about themselves, that's when you start to move down the path of success and becoming great. It's so much more valuable than cutting to the chase or badgering a customer with a long list of questions that ultimately feel more like they are about what you need than a way to learn how to help and support them.

## It's Not a Performance

One bad habit that some salespeople have is called "showing up and throwing up." That's when a salesperson gets so focused on giving their presentation that they don't check in with the customer at all. They don't find out whether what they're saying is actually answering their questions or addressing their problems. They go into a sort of "performance mode" where all they do is talk, and they can't absorb any feedback from the customer. Usually, the customer doesn't have any room to respond.

I worked at a company with a very anxious salesperson named Martin. His fears about being liked and being good at his job got in the way of him genuinely connecting with people. I had gotten feedback from his manager that he was coming across in his sales calls as too impersonal, even robotic. Everything about the way he related to customers made it seem like all he was there for was the transaction. He wasn't approaching customers with authenticity and curiosity, and he would start talking a million miles an hour without them being able to get a word in. It was much more like he was talking at people than with people. Things he said in most of his calls didn't quite seem aligned to the situation or the customer. He was putting in the work, doing the activities, but his execution was at best a little off and at worst losing the company customers.

Rather than telling Martin to do better, I decided to get a better view of that 90 percent of his iceberg that was underwater. I needed to learn what was going on with him, what was deeper than what his manager was observing in Martin's sales calls.

"Martin, on a scale of one to ten, one being low and ten being high, how would you rate yourself on the connection you have with your leads and customers?" I asked him.

"I'd say a six," he said.

"How would you rate yourself when you're with your wife or your friends or your family?"

"Definitely an eight to a ten."

"That's a big difference. What's that about? What's getting in the way of you connecting with people in the same way you do with your friends and family?"

For a while, Martin sat and thought about it.

"Actually, I think I know what it is," he finally said. "I used to wait tables, and when I was doing that, I approached customers in a completely different way than I am supposed to in this job."

Basically, Martin's experience with customers when he was waiting tables was a kind of performance. In his restaurant jobs, he had scripts for how to present the specials for the day, how to take orders, and how to politely check in during different parts of the meal. Everything he did was transactional, delivering information in exchange for food orders, bringing the orders to the customers, and eventually accepting money to close out the transaction. As soon as he interacted with diners, he was on a stage and they were the audience. This was not the sort of person-to-person dialogue that was needed in his current sales position.

It wasn't really the type of interaction he needed to be a great server either. Because he was nervous to talk to the restaurant's customers, he would operate very mechanically, very scripted, very copy-paste. He was the type of server you'd forget about the next day rather than the kind you'd be excited to see again. Using those skills wouldn't have helped him earn more tips; it certainly wasn't going to help him get better at his current sales job.

"Okay, so when you're on a call with a customer in your current position, do you still see yourself in waiter's clothes?"

"I guess I do," Martin said.

When Martin adopted what we started calling his "waiter voice," it kept the person he was speaking to at arm's length. It's pretty difficult to build a relationship with someone when you feel like you are performing every time you talk to them, that they are in the audience and you are on the stage. In the solutions-based sales he was doing now, he was specifically supposed to be building rapport. It was hard to do that if he was merely giving his customers a presentation instead of having a conversation with them, especially if he never gave them a chance to respond to him.

We needed to move the dial from where it was now to the same level of connection that he felt with his friends and family. One thing I knew about Martin was that he enjoyed activities like skiing, hiking, and fly-fishing. We started there.

"What if you imagined a customer you spoke with as a friend in your Subaru heading to go skiing?" I suggested. "Or someone you met at a waterfall at the end of a hiking trip and you both are looking at this amazing view and start talking about the shared experience? Or a friend you are planning a fly-fishing trip with where you need to understand who does what and when to make a successful experience for the both of you? Instead of putting on a show for them, you could think about it as inviting them along on a journey with you."

"I can try that," he said with a hopeful smile.

I smiled too. "Great. So, what would you ask me if we were going to plan a trip together?"

From the way he lit up, he obviously got it. "I guess I would first want to understand what you wanted out of the trip, where you wanted to go, and what you wanted to do."

"Perfect," I said. "Try that next time you talk to a customer."

With practice, Martin started showing up more authentically. He started finding more in common with his customers, and that made it easier for him to relax around them. It helped him feel like he was making more human connections, and he finally started building rapport, getting more appointments, and generating more proposals.

You might feel a lot of comfort from having your discovery questions, list of features and benefits, and even prepared responses to every objection at the ready. But when you're building rapport, those aren't the tools you need. Spitting out as much information as possible as fast as possible won't help you build rapport. Trying to convince your customer by overcoming objections won't either. In fact, all of this will probably do the opposite and alienate your customer. Next time you interact with a customer, I invite you to slow down and treat them as someone on a journey with you, as a collaboration partner with you as their co-pilot.

## Show Up as Yourself, and Your Customers Will Too

The process of building rapport is your biggest opportunity to explore the icebergs that surround you. *Rapport* is not a meaningless buzzword or a reminder to be on your best behavior (even though, yeah, you should probably do that too). It's a reminder that this is a process of building relationships with your customers that go beyond the 10 percent of what you can see at first.

Once you've given a customer a picture of how a meeting will go and created a comfortable environment for them, keep hanging out in that place of curiosity and connection. This is where you stay present with them as your genuine self. This is also where many salespeople can get nervous or feel uncomfortable.

But putting yourself out there and being real is where your power lies. Being genuine and showing who you really are creates an environment where others can do the same. Get comfortable revealing more and more of your iceberg if you want others to do so as well. Maybe you have triggers from your past, maybe from when you were a kid and you felt people judged you or maybe from prior sales managers who micromanaged you or simply gave you bad advice.

You may have some anxiety about showing up authentically. You might even get triggered when someone simply suggests that you show up authentically. That's all okay. This is a journey. You are literally going from one state to another. From being good to being great.

So, let your customers get to know you by showing them some of your iceberg and being curious and open. In doing so, you are creating the space to share their needs and ask their questions. This best practice is the key to Iceberg Selling, and as you share, so will your customers. And it will be this sharing that gives you and them insights into how best to work together.

# Best Practice #4—
# Test for Success

Use the rapport you've built to brainstorm, suggest, and co-create solutions with your customer.

- Get on the same side of the table and set yourself up for collaboration rather than focusing on "winning" their business.

- Take chances by floating ideas that help you gain insight and get closer to a solution.

- Co-create solutions that work for everyone based on the rapport you've built and feedback from the ideas you have shared.

**Once you've built rapport, you come to one of my most** favorite parts of any sales call. This is the part where you start sharing ideas and creating solutions alongside your customer. If you've really been listening to what they've said, if you've stayed curious and present with them, you very likely have some ideas about how you can help them.

By this point in the call, you will have created a safe place for both of you to be creative without feeling like you're on rival teams. Nobody is there for a "gotcha" moment, and nobody is out to win against the other person. It should be obvious to them that you really want to help, and they'll trust you enough to hear what you can offer.

If you have architected your meeting and invited them to collaborate effectively, the customer will know that they can be honest with you and that you haven't set any traps. It takes a ton of pressure off both of you, and chances are, it'll cause less anxiety on sales calls.

But to get to this place of trust and co-creation, you need to see the shape and size of your customer's iceberg. To really get to that point, you also need to let go of some of the less effective and even negative tactics you've learned about sales.

## Get on the Same Side of the Table

Say there's a salesperson who sells flooring to homeowners with what he thinks is a great tactic. He'll walk around the house with a clipboard as the customer watches, carefully looking into every corner but not really engaging the customer. Then he'll turn around, pen in his hand, and say, "What's your budget?"

He insists that everyone has a budget and that anyone who says they don't is lying. He refuses to say anything else until they've given him a number. It's like his pro-wrestling finishing move.

Not only is this whole approach creating an unneeded confrontation, it doesn't take into account all the opportunities that come from brainstorming solutions alongside the customer rather than against them. It also can make a customer feel very unsafe because now they're afraid that if they tell him a number that's too high, they're going to end up overpaying, and a number too low, they are going to be judged as foolish or unrealistic. He has centered the whole interaction around pricing rather than value, on a transaction rather than a relationship.

There was a time when I was interviewing for different sales jobs, and I kept finding that one of the biggest criteria for them was being good at persuasion. I would take assessments at professional services firms, and all the questions were about persuasion. It always rubbed me the wrong way.

For me, persuasion is forcing. It equals manipulation. But I bet you've heard that it's an important trait for a salesperson as much as I have. It's based on conflict, where you're just trying to get someone to say yes. Then you win, and the other person loses. It's like you're sitting across the table from one another playing poker instead of sitting side-by-side and building the coolest house of cards ever.

What we're trying to get away from with Iceberg Selling is that adversarial approach. With Iceberg Selling, you don't need to rely on all those hard-edged *Glengarry Glen Ross* tactics.

That goes for all the common rules you've probably heard before, like whoever speaks first loses, whoever asks the most questions wins, and you have to know how to overcome every objection.

I'm telling you to throw all that us-versus-them stuff out of your mind. Instead, continue to focus on rapport building. Then, when it comes time to offer solutions, think about it as testing for success rather than persuading them or performing some type of sales judo.

The flooring salesperson I talked about earlier had a lot of opportunities to explore his customer's iceberg. He could have started by asking questions about their life and why they're looking for new flooring. What does a typical day look like for them? And what do they plan to do with their house? They might plan to have kids or get another dog. Maybe they want to flip the house and sell it in a year. Those are completely different needs that will affect the buying decision, and the salesperson will make suggestions based on solving their problems rather than on price.

Creating a context where you can safely and comfortably brainstorm with your customer involves vulnerability on both of your parts—but you need to lead the way. You need to talk as if money weren't an object, so you can think big, then modify everything to fit whatever the actual budget might be. If you or the customer don't trust one another to talk about money, then you can't take a good long look at all the possibilities. Fear puts major limits on how much you can imagine. This fear can be of seeming like a pushy salesperson, the fear that if you talk price, somehow you are no longer building rapport and are ruining the connection you've made. It can be your customer's fear that if they share their budget, somehow they are going to be tricked or taken less seriously. Fear in the selling process can show up in a lot of different ways, but I heavily encourage you to overcome whatever fear you might have and move forward with honest, collaborative dialogue.

Something that is helpful to both you and the customer is to bring back a technique I taught you as part of Best Practice #2. Tell your customer exactly what you are going to do in this section of the sales call.

You're asking for permission to take a risk, simply to float some ideas that enable you both to continue to work together. You are asking them to co-create a solution and possible next steps. This part is magic. It creates a safe place where everyone can imagine possibilities. But too often, we as salespeople forget to create this context and we blurt out a series of solutions. When we do this, it can feel like we are putting our customer on the spot—like we just gave them a pop quiz and they immediately need to come up with the answer. I don't know about you, but I never enjoyed pop quizzes in school. Most likely, your customers didn't either.

Instead of jumping right to a solution, you can say something like this to show your understanding of your customer and what they are looking to achieve and imagine a path forward.

"I have an idea—as a next step, could I share back what I think I heard you say? From there, it would be great if I could share some brainstorms to see if some of the ideas I have might be a fit. And if not, maybe we could just walk through them until we find something that makes sense for you. Would that work?"

In my experience, if there is enough trust and rapport between the two of you, then your customer will welcome this type of next step. Just remember, they are investing time with you so that you can learn about the problem they are looking to solve, then bring them a solution. Then, they can review that solution and ultimately decide whether it will get them where they need and want to go.

## Take Chances

As you navigate Iceberg Selling, you can't plow ahead to offer one solution and one solution only. You need to create a dialogue, putting ideas out to gain feedback, then adjusting based on that feedback. Ship captains use tools like sonar to find what icebergs they might not have seen or noticed on their navigation instruments. Sonar bounces signals off the icebergs to show their size and shape. That feedback helps captains figure out how to move forward.

Your customer's feedback on your ideas will show you when you should pivot and in which direction you should go.

Once the ideas start flowing, putting something out there is a way to open conversations and explore possibilities, even if you think it might be a little too over-the-top or not 100 percent correct. The worst that someone can do in response is to say no, but a no to one idea isn't the end of the conversation when you're in brainstorming mode. Not if you've agreed to collaborate on a solution.

If you're nervous about putting things out there, remember that you have experiences with the solutions they need—your product or service. You can draw comparisons to people you have worked with in the past who have had problems like theirs. You can point out what is different about their problems, and that will show them that you've been listening and that you understand them.

But the fact remains, you must put yourself out there and take chances to see what sticks.

At this point, you're also testing to make sure that you have the full picture of their iceberg too. There might be something that you missed along the way, a problem they need solved that either you didn't catch or they forgot to tell you. Do not be afraid to ask them to repeat themselves or clarify. You're not showing weakness; you're showing interest, engagement, and professionalism. You're asking for more information because you are curious and you want to see the whole shape of their problem. Asking to understand something better shows you are in their world and want to be of service to them. If your customer is nervous about sharing their reality, stepping forward to share more about yours will make them feel more confident and comfortable about sharing too.

By putting out those sonar signals, you get feedback, and you keep offering solutions. Test as you go, float ideas, and stay in possibility and solution. You will keep seeing where you can add value, and by seeing more and more of their iceberg, you will learn how you can make that value clear to them.

It reminds me of a story from when my son was young. Like most kids that age, he loved dump trucks, construction sites, and planes. My dad was over for a visit, and I invited him on the field trip I was about to take with my son.

"Do you want to go to the airport with me and Sam to watch planes take off?"

"I don't think so—I've already seen airplanes take off," he said.

"Let me rephrase that," I said. "Do you want to go to the airport and watch your three-year-old grandson experience planes landing and taking off?"

"Oh, that could be fun."

Reframing the situation in a way that helped my dad see the value of a trip to the airport made him realize he wanted something he didn't think he wanted before. And it was something that he genuinely wanted to do—to experience the delight of his grandson.

You might be worried that you'll suggest something that is outside the scope or a budget they named at the beginning, or you might be afraid that the idea you're giving them is too out there. But after all the rapport you've built and the brainstorming context you have set, you can't be sure that their attitudes haven't changed unless you ask. Even if they said in the beginning that they were making their decision based on price, your conversation may have made them realize they are looking for something bigger. You may have shown them options they didn't know were possible and now really want. If you have floated your ideas in ways that present value to them, you can work together to find a solution that works for both of you.

When I had a discovery call with the owner of a manufacturing company, we started our conversation by getting an idea of what he needed. He told me what his current state was and what he wanted his future state to look like. It was a great exercise for him to get clear on what he really wanted, and it was a great way for me to learn more about the rest of his iceberg. He wanted to increase his sales by finding more wholesale opportunities and building a two-part sales organization. One part would be to do business development and account acquisition, and the other would cover account management to increase retention and account growth.

Soon, we transitioned to a phase of the call that was part discovery and part brainstorming. He'd share another element of his company and vision, and I would repeat it back to him to make sure I fully understood. Then I would share brainstorms as well as solutions I had provided other past clients, asking him what he thought of the ideas. This went back and forth for twenty minutes, and by the end of the call, a variety of possible solutions began to form. The conversation then moved into curiosity about how these solutions would be executed, what he'd need internally to make them happen, and how my team and I would work within his organization.

We had done it. We had worked together to discover, explore, and ultimately come up with solutions to achieve what he really wanted for his company. Little by little, we could both see a more complete view of the iceberg of his project.

"This was a great call, Karl. I really appreciate it. I wish I would have reached out sooner!" he said near the end of the call.

I had invited him into a conversation, worked collaboratively to discover what he wanted his future reality to be, then worked as a team to co-create solutions and gauge those solutions for fit. All of it was built up as coming to an agreement together rather than as a one-sided presentation. I gave him a wide range of options to help him find something that worked for him, and we still worked within his budget and timelines.

Never forget that you are the person steering this ship. You are the one with the expertise. You can draw on your experience with previous projects and share what solutions worked for them with your customer. You are your customer's guide, and if you have ideas for solutions that could bring value to them, say something.

Testing ideas and solutions in front of your customer might feel like a completely natural collaboration. Other times it might feel more like a game of Chutes and Ladders, where when you've climbed a little higher, you go right back down. But that's okay, and it's part of the process of going from good to great. The most important thing is that you are in discovery mode, so you can work as a team with your customer to bring forth solutions that are best for them.

## Co-Create a Solution

You're leading the conversation, sending out the sonar signals, and listening for feedback from the customer. And since you're the expert on your offerings, you're going to be the person who comes up with the range of solutions they can choose from. If you come up with something on your own and then ask the customer to say yes to it, the chances of it sticking are a lot lower. However, if they arrive at the outcome with you, you have created the solution together. It belongs to them as much as it belongs to you, and they will be more invested in it. This is co-creation at its best.

In co-creation, your customer will be more likely to say, "Yes, this is exactly what I wanted to do."

When I tell a customer what to do, when I give them an answer they didn't help create, I have a higher risk of getting stuck in the check-in zone and even ghosted. Brainstorming without the customer's feedback is not co-creation; it's more like writing a prescription for what they need. Your customer probably won't want to just take whatever medicine you say they should. Simply being told what to do doesn't feel safe, and it certainly doesn't inspire action. That's why it's so important they be a part of brainstorming—why you want their feedback when you float ideas in their direction.

Earlier in this chapter, I named some of the common sales "rules" that get in the way of connecting with customers and create more of a transactional or even combative sales approach. One of them is overcoming objections, something you've likely been told is critical to closing a sale.

While understanding your customer's concerns is vital to understanding their iceberg and navigating to their desired state, value is created in how you learn about these concerns and react to them.

I once worked with a company with a software platform that was sold to universities. There were several common questions that customers raised, especially whether the platform complied with the Americans with Disabilities Act and how the technology would meet the university's cybersecurity requirements.

In the old model, a salesperson would have a whole script to "overcome objections" that came up multiple times. But this software company came at it from a different perspective. When their specifications and the school's requirements weren't 100 percent aligned, instead of getting sucked into a debate and trying to overcome the school's objections, they would suggest a working session that would bring in all the stakeholders. They would welcome questions so everything could be addressed all at once, and everyone who was involved would be educated and feel far more secure with the choices they were making. Salespeople at the software company built this Q&A session into their sales process and brought it up as an option even before the customers did. Schools loved it as there was a step in the evaluation cycle that enabled them to bring their concerns to a working session where their voices were heard and respected. The tech company could use the session to share their best practices and ways other schools had dealt with similar issues. It also enabled solution and alignment on next steps, helping to remove the check-in zone, getting ghosted, and a stretched-out sales cycle.

Sometimes co-creating solutions takes more than one meeting, and that's okay. I've started out calls with a solution that didn't work, then ended those calls with completely different solutions after brainstorming, taking chances, and co-creating something uniquely suited to the customer I was working with. It's not a disaster if your first idea isn't the one your customer chooses. It's just an opener. When an idea you have doesn't work for them, that's your cue to invite the customer to express more of what they need. Often that will rule out some of the ideas you offer and will bring you both to a satisfying answer much more quickly. After that period of brainstorming and processing, you'll be on the same side of the table, looking at a solution that you've cooperated to build.

## Moving Forward Together

At this point, you and your customer are in sync. You have collaborated enough to chart out a clear vision of the direction you want to take. Together, you've explored the iceberg of the problem in question and gauged the shape of it. If it seems like you're a good fit for each other, it's time for you to find the next steps that will take you from where you're standing right now to getting into the solution you discussed, and ultimately closing the sale.

This is the point where a lot of salespeople get stuck in the check-in zone. In the next chapter, I'll give you some advice on how to make it more likely you can act on the solution you have co-created.

# Best Practice #5—
# Set Next Steps

The experience you've created doesn't stop at the end of your meeting. Keep your drivership mindset and come to an agreement with your customer about what comes next.

- Stay out of your head. Recognize that having next steps serves your customer and you are offering guidance that will make their life better.

- Act now for success later, even if that means walking away.

- Always schedule the next meeting, no matter what, while you're in your current meeting. This makes it less likely you'll get stuck in the check-in zone.

You've done your research, made all the preparations, built rapport, and co-created a solution with the customer. Awesome. You've nailed the first four best practices.

This is often where we say, "All right! That was a great call! They want to work with me. Now all I've got to do is send them a proposal, and we're good to go."

Sorry, but you're not done yet. There's still one more thing to do before you end the meeting. You've architected this experience up until now, and it doesn't stop with this conversation. If you don't create your next steps right away, you run a major risk of getting stuck in the check-in zone. Nobody wants to be there. All this great connection and rapport you've built could start slipping away.

It's counterintuitive, because I think a lot of us think that if we've had a good call, taking out the calendar and talking about next steps is too "salesy." Suddenly, you aren't their collaborator. You're a person who came here to sell something to them. Salespeople worry that taking action like this will make their customer not want to talk to them anymore. They think it will ruin everything they've worked so hard to create.

I can say with confidence that the opposite is true.

If you have gotten this far, you've already shown your customer the value of what you have to offer. They already know you are guiding them forward and have taken stock of every iceberg around you. Continuing to apply your drivership mindset is actually of service to them as you continue to move forward together.

## Stay Out of Your Head

The truth is that, as salespeople, we have a lot of head trash around sales. These negative, unhelpful thoughts often turn up at the most inconvenient times, specifically, when we're trying to close business with a customer and set up our next steps.

Take, for example, an entrepreneur who founded a tech startup and who I met at one of my workshops. We'll call him Tim. It was right after I finished the workshop and was getting ready to go to the airport that he came up to me and asked if I did sales coaching. Since I had a good amount of time before my flight home, I asked him if he wanted to talk then and there about whatever was going on.

Tim had raised funding and had introductions to a list of great potential customers. He had met with many of these customers and done well creating dialogue and showcasing his solution. But he had a closing problem. It seemed like everything went well right up to the close; then things would fall apart. He'd meet his ideal customer, have a great initial conversation, come in for a presentation, meet an engaged audience, and then nothing. It was a problem with those final ten yards before he could get the ball into the end zone and score a touchdown or, in this case, close a sale.

He and I started to go deep. I asked him for examples and to share the core steps of his sales process. Consulting is a lot like Iceberg Selling. Success comes from exploring and seeing more and more of the iceberg.

The early steps of his sales process were about discovery, sharing his solution, and demonstrating how his solutions solved problems and enabled tech teams to be more efficient. All his initial steps seemed great to me. I appreciated Tim's openness. He was clearly passionate about his solution and was a domain expert who had solved a major issue. The value of his solution was real and relevant. Then we started to explore what would happen after the presentation, after he would get into conversations with his potential customers about features, functionalities, and use cases. As he told it, these potential customers would be right there with him, in agreement over how his solutions could support their teams. That was when things would go sideways—right there during that step from people agreeing with the value of his solution to them implementing his solution.

"Do you like sales?" I asked Tim.

Tim paused and then awkwardly said, "No, I hate it."

Next, I asked him what he thought sales was.

"It's convincing someone to do something," he said. "It makes me feel uncomfortable. I don't like doing it."

"Tim," I said, "I have good news for you. That's not sales."

There was a physical show of relief on his face, but he still seemed nervous.

"I know we just met today, but in the workshop, I observed a few things about you based on the questions you asked me in front of the group and the stories you told," I said. "I want to go out on a limb here, take a chance, but I might be about to open up something deep for you. Are you okay with that?"

Tim cautiously agreed.

"Okay...good. So, you told a few stories in the session today about getting in front of companies that could be really good fits for your solution. In all those stories, you left the meeting thinking it went well, and then nothing ever happened. But throughout the workshop today, you also told a couple stories about your father—how you grew up in his business, how he was a tough business owner, and how much you admired what he built and how he did it. Does that sound right?"

Tim agreed.

"Now, I want to ask you a heavy question. What I also observed when you told stories about your dad is it felt like stories about the past, like maybe you had lost your father. Did your father pass away recently?"

Tim froze. His eyes got watery. That answered the question for me even before he nodded.

"We all have triggers from past experiences," I affirmed. "So, I want to ask you another question. It's going to be about your dad, and it might be a little hard for you. Are you still good if we keep talking about all of this?"

Another nod.

"What did your father think of people in sales?"

Tim took a moment to answer.

"He didn't like them. He didn't like people telling him what he should or shouldn't do or what he should or shouldn't think. He didn't like feeling sold to."

I gave Tim a slight smile and thanked him. Then I asked, "When you sell, do you feel you are letting your dad down? Or being someone he wouldn't want you to be?"

Tim's eyes welled up again, and we sat there for a moment. A big piece of iceberg had revealed itself.

Finally, I said, "It's okay, Tim. You don't need to sell the way you think you 'should' or in a way you think would make your dad judge you. You can sell in a way that is right for you. From what I've learned about you, I think it's as simple as asking the tech customers you meet with if they'd be open to trying out your solution with their team. All you probably need to do is invite them into your solution and ask them to give feedback."

I told him that, from there, one of two things would happen. He would either learn that he needed to keep modifying his product until it was right based on what they said or the companies would see the value and want to move forward with him and invest in his solution.

That day, Tim changed his life. That day, Tim realized that sales isn't a bunch of words you say to magically convince someone to do something. He realized sales is about learning and understanding people. And once you understand someone's problems and can show them a path to what they need, it's up to them to choose whether they want to take that journey with you.

As I wrapped up with Tim, I pointed out that he was a phenomenal entrepreneur and had developed a relevant and high-value solution. When he talked to other engineers about what he had created, he showed up with passion and energy. Continuing to bring that passion and energy into an invitation for his potential customer to try out his offering would be of service to them and to his company.

"Letting them try it, then asking for your feedback, makes it so you're talking to them like a peer instead of talking across the table at them—like you're separate from them and only trying to make them say yes," I said.

After our conversation, Tim looked like a tremendous weight had been taken off his shoulders. Even better, in my follow-up calls and in his social media feeds, I heard about and saw his success.

When you take a minute to think about it, you'll realize that our culture, and often the people in our lives, have given us a lot of mixed messages about what sales really is. We all probably have our own experiences and stories here. I would like to share one of mine with you.

When I was in my twenties, I went with my father and younger sister to a local dealership to find her a used car. It was right after I had gotten my first real sales job—the one in the financial services company I told you about earlier in the book. We found the car my sister wanted, and then the three of us found ourselves in the sales manager's office, working on the deal. The sales manager and the sales guy who took us on the test-drive were telling my dad about the car, its history, its safety features, and how they had determined the price.

They were also explaining why the car could be a good fit for my sister when she went off to college.

My dad leaned back in his chair and said, "Why should I believe any of this? You just want to sell me a car. You're used-car salesmen!"

I remember the salespeople's expressions when my dad said that. I also remember how I felt for them and for myself. It was unnecessary, incorrect, and mean. The salespeople were doing their job, and doing a good job, if you asked me!

For years, that experience added to my personal head trash, but over time, I realized it was just that—trash. To overcome that feeling, I invite you to do what I did: realize that sales is a profession with a ton of value. Like I said at the beginning of this book, salespeople are great at listening to people and connecting with them. We create visions and make them accessible, then meet people on their level to guide them to that reality.

We are professionals, we are guides, we are the people who make changes and move things forward. We create value and make sure that value is aligned with what our customers need and want.

If you have your own story that creates head trash for you, I invite you now to let it go and shift your mindset. Remember that you're here to help people. In fact, you've probably already helped lots of people by now. If you're authentic and they're a good fit, they won't have buyer's remorse or think of you as manipulative. They're going to be grateful that you steered them into a solution that you co-created together.

## Focus on the Right Fit

If you've co-created a solution, you'll know what the next step is. So, don't wait to bring that forward. It's your job to make what comes next as easy as possible for your client. Using your drivership mindset to guide them into working together means you'll start delivering value sooner, and sharing with them what they need to know to move forward will keep them standing in the same place and seeing the same things as you.

Also, as a good salesperson, you probably know what a bad fit looks like. If you are captaining a ship, you can't force your way over an iceberg. That's a good way to sink. Iceberg Sellers know that forcing things with someone who won't get value from a solution can be as damaging.

For a long time, I, like a lot of other salespeople, thought that I was supposed to close business no matter what. It was all about hitting the numbers, and everyone would make it work later. But an ends-justify-the-means attitude creates problems down the road. That leads to rushing, not asking the right questions, and missing out on that 90 percent of the iceberg that is below the water. Because, as we established at the beginning, icebergs are always bigger than you think at first glance.

Like most people, I thought I could use my sales powers for good. I developed a belief that, if I could convince someone to buy from us, then they were automatically a good fit. To me, if I could sell something, I should sell it.

I'm always reminded of a story from when I ran a digital agency focused on building highly interactive, high-profile websites. We had received a referral from a snowboard brand we worked with for an up-and-coming ski brand. The ski brand had a great product and, on the surface, seemed like an amazing fit.

As we got into the project, we realized there was a huge misalignment. Our business was based on understanding a client's brand and then creating an experiential website based on our interpretation of their vision—a co-creation of strategies and design elements. Instead of employing our creativity and technical expertise, this company wanted a technical team that would create the site they wanted—no questions asked. They wanted us to design and program a website based on their napkin-drawn designs. That wasn't how we operated.

When I think back, the misalignment was obvious from the start. An older Karl would have passed on the opportunity, most likely referring it to another agency that was a better fit. The younger Karl moved forward with the relationship. Ultimately, both parties lost. My company put in a ton of work, went over budget trying to please them, and ultimately went upside down with hours (not to mention how we frustrated the entire team, from project management, to design, to development). The client ended up with a website they didn't want and didn't use. While it's water under the bridge, the old pair of their skis in my garage is a nice reminder of what not to do.

As I learned more about sales, met and was of service to more customers, and practiced co-creating solutions, I discovered that meeting someone on their level sometimes means walking away from a deal. That's a solution in itself. It frees up the customer to find something that works better for them, and it helps you do the same thing for your company.

As an Iceberg Seller, you're using a mindset of looking at the big picture rather than just making the transaction. Making a decision based on that 90 percent below the surface can sometimes mean turning around and going the other way. That's the opposite of a failure. Saying no to the wrong fit frees everyone up for better outcomes in the long run.

## Always Schedule Your Next Meeting

If you're one of the many people who worry that talking about making the next appointment will turn you from a person into a salesperson, I've got good news. If you've been following the Iceberg Selling best practices, your customers will be grateful for your drivership mindset. That's because you will have told everyone attending the meeting exactly what will happen at the end. There will be no surprise. You will be doing what you already told them you'd do and what you both agreed to at the beginning of your call.

And on top of that, here's something kind of counterintuitive: You might think that if you're doing business with someone with a high-level job title, you shouldn't push them or manage them to the next step. Actually, the more senior the person you're dealing with, the more guiding them through the process of next steps is a huge service to them. Their inbox is always overflowing, their Slack channels are blowing up, they're buried in notifications. If you haven't given them a clear next step, they may not get back to you. They will move on to their next priority, leaving you stuck in a check-in zone that could be both hard and time-consuming to climb out of.

So, remember, even with someone who may intimidate you a little, you're a necessary guide. Once you've gotten buy-in on a course of action, you can say something like this:

"I think this was a great call. I'm going to work on this proposal, and could we get something on the calendar right now for Thursday or Friday, so I can walk you through it? That way, if there are any changes, I can make them in real time."

They probably won't hesitate to pull their calendars out. Being proactive like this is the best way to avoid the check-in zone and the best way to support your customer and yourself. It's of service to everyone.

Plus, things are always going to happen that you can't predict. Even with lots of experience, you can still sometimes get stuck in a check-in zone if you haven't been proactive with future appointments.

I finished a great call one day with the president of a large manufacturing company, and I was so confident about where we'd landed and the rapport we had built that I completely forgot to put something on the calendar. But I wasn't super concerned. He had already said yes on the call, and he wanted to move forward with the solution we had co-created. All I had to do was send him the contract.

I sent him the contract. Time passed, and I didn't hear back.

If something like this happens to you, this is the point where you start to get nervous. Your mind starts playing tricks on you. No matter how well the call went, you start wondering whether you were imagining all the positive signs you saw. Even if they said yes, you worry that they've changed their mind. Again, this is where you start thinking about the deal rather than the relationship. And especially if you're trying to meet a quota on a deadline, you may go back to that place of having transaction tunnel vision. And that's not what Iceberg Selling is all about.

Eventually, we reconnected, and the CEO signed the contract. But that was after eight weeks of following up.

It's always better if you create a backstop, if you already have a time on everyone's calendar to stay in proactive and constructive conversation. Then you won't have to go back and forth for weeks, waiting for paperwork to be signed that you could have taken care of on a short call.

## Iceberg Selling Makes Closing Natural

In sales 101, people learn tactics where they ask leading questions that get as many yeses as possible. It's all about nudging the customer closer and closer to a transaction:

"Is this checking off all the boxes for you?"

"Have we answered all your questions today?"

"Is this the solution you're looking for?"

"Are you thinking you might want to move forward?"

You're already a good salesperson, so you don't need me to tell you how to close deals. But with Iceberg Selling, you aren't focused on saying the magic words that make anyone buy from you. This isn't like one of those "hotshot salesperson" movies we've all seen and probably referenced now and again. This is something better, and it works.

Because the remarkable thing about closing when you are Iceberg Selling is, when you find the right fit, that customer will tell you they want to buy before you even ask them. Your customer will recognize you've got the solution they need. They will tell you they want to move forward. By the end of the call, if you've followed all the Iceberg Selling best practices, the right fit will be raring to go with a strong yes and agreement to next steps.

# Conclusion:
# Iceberg Selling
# Changes Everything

If you're anything like me (and since you're in sales, you probably are), you're always looking for the next rush. Closing deals is satisfying. It's addictive. You have proof of a job well done, and you're getting rewarded for it. The prime example is the rush you get when a customer says yes to a deal, but that's not the only way you can get it.

Iceberg Selling can give you a rush from the work you do as a salesperson even outside of the deal itself.

Being the captain of my ship, being of service, building rapport, and really being involved in someone else's success is also deeply satisfying. To me, that's because the rush of being a successful salesperson is all about feeling connected to others, feeling understood and valued. Sure, the satisfaction that comes from winning and making money makes a big difference to most of us, and if you use Iceberg Selling, you will definitely see higher numbers in your bank account. But being acknowledged and recognized and seen by others can make selling mean so much more.

It feels the way you might feel if you throw that eightieth birthday party for your dad and completely knock it out of the park. Or the way you do when your kid shows you their college acceptance letter after you've helped them through an intense application process. Or how you might feel after you planned out a one-of-a-kind road trip with your best friends and it's as amazing as everyone dreamed it would be.

You've architected, nurtured, and co-created something that improves the life of people you care about.

Iceberg Selling is all about caring about what's under the surface for your customers, caring about their needs. If you do it right, you get satisfaction from more than closing a deal. You've also created an amazing experience for someone, and they have recognized you and appreciated you for it. That is the experience of truly connecting with people, and that's what I've seen that most salespeople want to feel as they do their jobs.

Now, let me tell you what's going to happen when you start Iceberg Selling—and believe me when I tell you that you will start seeing results right away.

Let's start with your personal success.

You're going to make more money. You're going to close more deals. The customers you're talking to are actually going to tell you they're ready to buy, versus you asking them. Your whole way of closing is going to go from asking for the order to taking the order, because they're going to tell you they want it.

Then the next part is the success you will have in your relationships.

Your connections with your clients and colleagues will deepen, but so will much more. The effects of Iceberg Selling will also spill into your personal life. The more you look at everything as icebergs, the more you invest time in your customers, the more that behavior will become muscle memory. You'll start investing more time in all people—your spouse, your kids, your friends—going from a red-lined, too-busy person to someone who shows people around them you care. You'll be of more service to the people in your life. You'll make them feel heard and understood.

So, are you feeling energized? Charged? Ready to go? You can start Iceberg Selling right now.

Take a minute to focus one thing that stood out to you in the mindset shifts and the best practices of Iceberg Selling. Pick any of the things we talked about and apply them to your next sales action.

Drawn to one of the mindset changes (or all four of them)? Think about somebody you're supposed to follow up with, and instead of asking them, "Hey, think you might be ready to buy?" envision what you can do for them. Maybe you recently saw a documentary about something you know they're interested in or you tried an amazing restaurant near them and thought they might like to visit with their spouse. Send them a link. No ulterior motive. Just being of service and playing for lifetime value.

What about the people in your funnel or who you are meeting with at your next appointment? How can you change the way you show up with them to really own the experience? Is there a place in your work where you've become stuck in the passenger seat when you should be driving? How can you switch seats and take them where they really want to go.

Got a meeting coming up with a new client? Try doing a little more research than you normally would—even if it's just five or ten minutes more. See how much of a difference that makes in what you learn; how much more could you learn in twenty minutes or even an hour?

If you want to do a better job setting up for success, think about your past meetings. Are there any places where you find things going sideways? Consider why that is and if there's anything you can do to change the environment or the way you show up that will make things go more smoothly afterward.

If you want to build better rapport, start with this simple thought: What question do you wish your customer would ask you? Ask them that same question, and they'll probably turn right around and ask it back. You'll have shown them a little of your iceberg, and it's a pretty good bet that you'll get to see some of theirs in return. Then, once you've shown that curiosity, hold space to learn the answer.

Experiment with testing for success. How fun would it be if, on your next call, you ask the customer to brainstorm with you for ten minutes—no holds barred? Throw out a couple solutions and ask them what they would modify to make your ideas work better for them. Let them co-create with you.

Setting next steps is one of the most straightforward ways to implement Iceberg Selling. Take a minute before the end of your next call and say, "Before we go, can we get out our calendars and pick a time to continue this conversation?"

And if you've got analysis paralysis and are sitting there wondering whether you should even be in sales, start with the very first thing that we talked about:

Ask yourself, "What am I playing for?"

What motivates you? Maybe it's the money, or the rush, or the freedom, or (most likely) some combination of all those things. Maybe it's the impact that you can make on the people in your life—your family, your coworkers, your friends. Ask yourself what it would be like if all those things started benefiting from your shifting mindset and approach to sales. That strong *why* will help you create enough momentum to power you through the next hour, day, week, month, year, and beyond.

With Iceberg Selling, the impact you can make in your company and in the lives of the people who matter to you— including yourself—is limitless.

# Acknowledgments

Iceberg Selling starts with getting clarity around people and situations in our lives, and I never would have learned to do it without the community of people I interact with daily. I'm grateful to my family, friends, coaching clients, and others who have had the deep conversations with me that have helped me refine the concepts in Iceberg Selling. Thank you to all those who, by sharing their own experiences, have taught me how sales is not all about chasing money. It's about being of service to others and creating value for them, whether or not you get anything back.

Special thanks to Steve Halligan, Jason Hughes, Dave Jensen, Brad Kemp, Scott Landes, Anne Lawrence, Lynne Smithpeter, Brett Trainor, Benjamin Wood, and Jacob Wood for giving their feedback on early drafts of this book. Lastly, thanks to Emily Einolander for helping me bring forward the concept of Iceberg Selling in an accessible, professional way.

# About the Author

**Karl Becker has founded and run numerous companies** over the last thirty years and now runs Improving Sales Performance, a consultancy that supports sales organizations to build high-performing teams and achieve their revenue goals. He is the author of *Set Up to Win: Three Frameworks to a High-Performing Sales Organization* and *Sales & Marketing Alignment*. He has a BA in economics from Colorado College and an MBA from the University of Colorado Boulder. You can learn more about him and his work at improvingsales-performance.com.

Made in the USA
Las Vegas, NV
30 October 2024

10790115R00075